Simply
Christian

✝

Simply Christian

Why Christianity

Makes Sense

N. T. Wright

HarperOne
An Imprint of HarperCollins*Publishers*

HarperOne

First published in Great Britain in 2006 by Society for Promoting Christian Knowledge.

HarperCollins books may be purchased for educational, business, or sales promotional use. For information please write: Special Markets Department, HarperCollins Publishers, 10 East 53rd Street, New York, NY 10022.

HarperCollins Web site: http://www.harpercollins.com
HarperCollins®, ▲®, and HarperOne™ are
trademarks of HarperCollins Publishers.

Designed by Joseph Rutt

Library of Congress Cataloging-in-Publication Data
Wright, N. T. (Nicholas Thomas)
Simply Christian : why Christianity makes sense / N. T. Wright.—1st ed.
p. cm.
ISBN 978–0–06–192062–2
1. Christianity. I. Title.
BR121.3.W75   2006
230—dc22   2005055139

10 11 12 13 14 RRD(H) 10 9 8 7 6 5 4 3 2 1

For Joseph and Ella-Ruth

Contents

Part Three
Reflecting the Image

Introduction

There are two sorts of traveler. The first sets off in the general direction of the destination and is quite happy to figure things out on the way, to read the signposts, ask directions, and muddle through. The second wants to know in advance what the road will be like, where it changes from a country road to a busy multilane highway, how long it will take to complete the different sections, and so on.

Concertgoers are often like that, too. Some listeners prefer to allow the music to make its own impact, carrying them along from movement to movement without their knowing where it will go next. Others find greater enjoyment by reading a program note in advance so that they can anticipate what is to come and have a mental picture of the whole while listening to the parts as they unfold.

People who read books divide into more or less the same types. The first type can probably skip this introduction and go straight to the first chapter. The second type may like to know in advance more or less where we're going, how the music is shaped. This introduction is written for them.

My aim has been to describe what Christianity is all about, both to commend it to those outside the faith and to explain it to those inside. This is a massive task, and I make no pretense of having covered everything, or even of having faced all the questions some might expect in a book of this sort. What I have tried to do is to give the subject a particular shape, resulting in the book's threefold structure.

First, I have explored four areas which in today's world can be interpreted as "echoes of a voice": the longing for justice, the quest for spirituality, the hunger for relationships, and the delight in beauty. Each of these, I suggest, points beyond itself, though without in itself enabling us to deduce very much about the world except that it is a strange and exciting place. Part One of the book, with its four chapters, functions rather like the opening movement of a symphony: once you have heard these themes, the trick is to hold them in your mind while listening to the second and third movements, whose rather different tunes will gradually meet up with the opening ones, producing "echoes" of a different sort. The first part, in other words, raises questions which are then, bit by bit and not always directly, addressed and at least partially answered in what follows. I only ask that the reader should be patient, as the second and third parts unfold, in waiting to see how the book eventually ties itself together.

Part Two lays out the central Christian belief about God. Christians believe that there is one true and living God, and that this God, revealed in action in Jesus, is the God who called the Jewish people to be his agents in setting forward his plan to rescue and reshape his creation. We therefore spend a whole chapter (Chapter Six) in looking at the story and hopes of ancient Israel, before spending two chapters on Jesus and two on the Spirit. Gradually, as this part unfolds, we discover that the voice whose echoes we began to listen for in the first part becomes recognizable, as we reflect on the creator God who longs to put his world to rights; on the human being called Jesus who announced God's kingdom, died on a cross, and rose again; and on the Spirit, who blows like a powerful wind through the world and through human lives.

This leads naturally into Part Three, where I describe what it looks like in practice to follow this Jesus, to be energized by this Spirit, and above all to advance the plan of this creator God. Worship (including sacramental worship), prayer, and scripture launch us into thinking about "the church," seen not as a building and not even so much as an institution, but as the company of all those who believe in the God we see in Jesus and who are struggling to follow him.

In particular, I explore the question of what the church is there *for*. The point of following Jesus isn't simply so that we can be sure of going to a better place than this after we die. Our future beyond death is enormously important, but the nature of the Christian hope is such that it plays back into the present life. We're called, here and now, to be instruments of God's new creation, the world-put-to-rights which has already been launched in Jesus and of which Jesus's followers are supposed to be not simply beneficiaries but also agents. This provides a new way of coming at various topics, not least prayer and Christian behavior. And this in turn enables us, as the book reaches its conclusion, to find the "echoes" of the first part coming back again, not now as hints of a God we might learn to know for ourselves, but as key elements of the Christian calling to work for his kingdom within the world.

This has been an exciting book to write, not least because it is quite personal; but in those terms it is, as it were, back to front. I have been a worshipping, praying, and Bible-reading Christian (often muddled and getting things wrong, but hanging in there) all my life, so that in a sense Part Three is where I began. I have spent much of my professional life studying Jesus historically and theologically, as well as trying to follow him personally, and Part Two embodies that multilayered quest. But, as I have done so, I have found that the issues in Part One have become more and more insistent and important. To take the first and most obvious example, the more I've learned about Jesus, the more I've discovered about God's passion to put the world to rights. And at that point I have also discovered that the things to which my study of Jesus has pointed me—the "echoes of a voice" in Part One—are among the things which the postmodern, post-Christian, and now increasingly postsecular world cannot escape as questions—strange signposts pointing beyond the landscape of our contemporary culture and out into the unknown.

I haven't attempted in these pages to differentiate between the many different varieties of Christianity, but have tried to speak of that which is, at their best, common to all. The book isn't "Anglican," "Catholic," "Protestant," or "Orthodox," but simply Christian. I have also attempted to keep what must be said as straightforward and clear as I can, so that those coming to the subject for the first time won't get stuck in a jungle of technical terms. Being a Christian in today's world is, of course, anything but simple. But there is a time for trying to say, as simply as possible, what it's all about, and this seems to me that sort of a time.

Between writing the first draft of this book and preparing it for publication, I had the joy of welcoming my first two grandchildren into the world. I dedicate the book to Joseph and Ella-Ruth, with the hope and prayer that they and their generation may come to hear the voice whose echoes we trace in the first part, to know the Jesus we meet in the second, and to live in and for the new creation we explore in the third.

Simply
Christian

Part One

Echoes of a Voice

One

Putting the World to Rights

I had a dream the other night, a powerful and interesting dream And the really frustrating thing about it is that I can't remember what it was about. I had a flash of it as I woke up, enough to make me think how extraordinary and meaningful it was; and then it was gone. And so, to misquote T. S. Eliot, I had the meaning but missed the experience.

Our passion for justice often seems like that. We dream the dream of justice. We glimpse, for a moment, a world at one, a world put to rights, a world where things work out, where societies function fairly and efficiently, where we not only know what we ought to do but actually do it. And then we wake up and come back to reality. But what are we hearing when we're dreaming that dream?

It's as though we can hear, not perhaps a voice itself, but the echo of a voice: a voice speaking with calm, healing authority, speaking about justice, about things being put to rights, about peace and hope and prosperity for all. The voice continues to echo in our imagination, our subconscious. We want to go back and listen to it again, but having woken up we can't get back into the dream. Other people sometimes tell us it was just a fantasy, and we're half-inclined to believe them, even though that condemns us to cynicism.

But the voice goes on, calling us, beckoning us, luring us to think that there might be such a thing as justice, as the world being put to rights, even though we find it so elusive. We're like moths trying to fly to the moon. We all know there's something called justice, but we can't quite get to it.

You can test this out easily. Go to any school or playgroup where the children are old enough to talk to each other. Listen to what they are saying. Pretty soon one child will say to another, or perhaps to a teacher: "That's not *fair!*"

You don't have to teach children about fairness and unfairness. A sense of justice comes with the kit of being human. We know about it, as we say, in our bones.

You fall off your bicycle and break your leg. You go to the hospital and they fix it. You stagger around on crutches for a while. Then, rather gingerly, you start to walk normally again. Pretty soon you've forgotten about the whole thing. You're back to normal. There *is* such a thing as putting something to rights, as fixing it, as getting it back on track. You can fix a broken leg, a broken toy, a broken television.

So why can't we fix injustice?

It isn't for want of trying. We have courts of law and magistrates and judges and lawyers in plenty. I used to live in a part of London where there was so much justice going on that it hurt—lawmakers, law enforcers, a Lord Chief Justice, a police headquarters, and, just a couple of miles away, enough barristers to run a battleship. (Though, since they would all be arguing with one another, the battleship might be going around in circles.) Other countries have similarly heavyweight organizations designed to make laws and implement them.

And yet we have a sense that justice itself slips through our fingers. Sometimes it works; often it doesn't. Innocent people get convicted; guilty people are let off. The bullies, and those who can bribe their way out of trouble, get away with wrongdoing—not always, but often enough for us to notice, and to wonder why.

People hurt others badly and walk away laughing. Victims don't always get compensated. Sometimes they spend the rest of their lives coping with sorrow, hurt, and bitterness.

The same thing is going on in the wider world. Countries invade other countries and get away with it. The rich use the power of their money to get even richer while the poor, who can't do anything about it, get even poorer. Most of us scratch our heads and wonder why, and then go out and buy another product whose profit goes to the rich company.

I don't want to be too despondent. There *is* such a thing as justice, and sometimes it comes out on top. Brutal tyrannies are overthrown. Apartheid was dismantled. Sometimes wise and creative leaders arise and people follow them into good and just actions. Serious criminals are sometimes caught, brought to trial, convicted, and punished. Things that are seriously wrong in society are sometimes put splendidly to rights. New projects give hope to the poor. Diplomats achieve solid and lasting peace. But just when you think it's safe to relax . . . it all goes wrong again.

And even though we can solve a few of the world's problems, at least temporarily, we know perfectly well that there are others we simply can't and won't.

Just after Christmas of 2004 an earthquake and tidal wave killed more than three times as many people in a single day as the total number of American soldiers who died in the entire Vietnam War. There are some things in our world, on our *planet,* which make us say, "That's not right!" even when there's nobody to blame. A tectonic plate's got to do what a tectonic plate's got to do. The earthquake wasn't caused by some wicked global capitalist, by a late-blossoming Marxist, or by a fundamentalist with a bomb. It just *happened.* And in that happening we see a world in pain, a world out of joint, a world where things occur which we seem powerless to make right.

The most telling examples are the ones closest to home. I have high moral standards. I have thought about them. I have preached about them. Good heavens, I have even written *books* about them.

And I still break them. The line between justice and injustice, between things being right and things not being right, can't be drawn between "us" and "them." It runs right down through the middle of each one of us. The ancient philosophers, not least Aristotle, saw this as a wrinkle in the system, a puzzle at several levels. We all know what we ought to do (give or take a few details); but we all manage, at least some of the time, not to do it.

Isn't this odd?

How does it happen that, on the one hand, we all share not just a sense that there is such a thing as justice, but a passion for it, a deep longing that things should be put to rights, a sense of out-of-jointness that goes on nagging and gnawing and sometimes screaming at us—and yet, on the other hand, after millennia of human struggle and searching and love and longing and hatred and hope and fussing and philosophizing, we still can't seem to get much closer to it than people did in the most ancient societies we can discover?

The Cry for Justice

Recent years have witnessed extravagant examples of human actions that have outraged our sense of justice. People sometimes talk as if the last fifty years have seen a decline in morality. But actually these have been some of the most morally sensitive, indeed moralistic, times in recorded history. People care, and care passionately, about the places where the world needs putting to rights.

Powerful generals sent millions to die in the trenches in the First World War, while they themselves lived in luxury behind the lines or back home. When we read the poets who found themselves caught up in that war, we sense behind their poignant puzzlement a smoldering anger at the folly and, yes, the injustice of it all. Why should it have happened? How can we put it to rights?

An explosive cocktail of ideologies sent millions to die in the gas chambers. Bits and pieces of religious prejudice, warped philosophies, fear of people who are "different," economic hardship, and the need for scapegoats were all mixed together by a brilliant demagogue who told people what at least some of them wanted to believe, and who demanded human sacrifices as the price of "progress." You only have to mention Hitler or the Holocaust to awaken the question: How did it happen? Where is justice? How can we get it? How can we put things right? And, in particular, How can we stop it from happening again?

But we can't, or so it seems. Nobody stopped the Turks from killing millions of Armenians from 1915 to 1917 (in fact, Hitler famously referred to this when he was encouraging his colleagues to kill Jews). Nobody stopped Tutsis and Hutus in Rwanda from killing each other in very large numbers in 1994. The world had said "Never again" after the Nazi Holocaust, but genocide *was* happening again, and we discovered to our horror that there was nothing we could do to stop it.

And then there was apartheid. Massive injustice was perpetrated against a very large population in South Africa for a very long time. Other countries, of course, had done similar things, but they had been more effective in squashing opposition. Think of the "reservations" for "Native Americans": I remember the shock when I saw an old "cowboys and Indians" movie and realized that when I was young, I—like most of my contemporaries—would have gone along unquestioningly with the assumption that cowboys were basically good and Indians basically bad. The world has woken up to the reality of racial prejudice since then; but getting rid of it is like squashing the air out of a balloon. You deal with one corner only to find it popping up somewhere else. The world got together over apartheid and said, "This won't do"; but at least some of the moral energy came from what the psychologists call *projection*—that is, condemning someone else for something we are doing ourselves. Rebuking someone on the other side of the world (while ignoring the same problems back home) is very convenient, and it provides a deep but spurious sense of moral satisfaction.

And now we have the new global evils: rampant, uncaring, and irresponsible materialism and capitalism on the one hand; raging, unthinking religious fundamentalism on the other. As one famous book puts it, we have "Jihad versus McWorld." (Whether there is such a thing as caring capitalism, or for that matter thoughtful fundamentalism, isn't the point at the moment.) This brings us back to where we were a few minutes ago. It doesn't take a Ph.D. in macroeconomics to know that if the rich are getting richer by the minute, and the poor poorer, there is something badly wrong.

Meanwhile, we all want a happy and secure home life. Dr. Johnson, the eighteenth-century conversationalist, once remarked that the aim and goal of all human endeavor is "to be happy at home." But in the Western world, and many other parts as well, homes and families are tearing themselves apart. The gentle art of being gentle—of kindness and forgiveness, sensitivity and thoughtfulness and generosity and humility and good old-fashioned love—have gone out of fashion. Ironically, everyone is demanding their "rights," and this demand is so shrill that it destroys one of the most basic "rights," if we can put it like that: the "right," or at least the longing and hope, to have a peaceful, stable, secure, and caring place to live, to be, to learn, and to flourish.

Once again people ask the question: Why is it like this? Does it *have* to be like this? Can things be put to rights, and if so how? Can the world be rescued? Can *we* be rescued?

And once again we find ourselves asking: Isn't it odd that it should be like that? Isn't it strange that we should all want things to be put to rights but can't seem to do it? And isn't the oddest thing of all the fact that I, myself, know what I ought to do but often don't do it?

A Voice, or a Dream?

There are three basic ways of explaining this sense of the echo of a voice, this call to justice, this dream of a world (and all of us within it) put to rights.

We can say, if we like, that it is indeed only a dream, a projection of childish fantasies, and that we have to get used to living in the world the way it is. Down that road we find Machiavelli and Nietzsche, the world of naked power and grabbing what you can get, the world where the only sin is to be caught.

Or we can say, if we like, that the dream is of a different world altogether, a world where we really belong, where everything is indeed put to rights, a world into which we can escape in our dreams in the present and hope to escape one day for good—but a world which has little purchase on the present world except that people who live in this one sometimes find themselves dreaming of that one. That approach leaves the unscrupulous bullies running this world, but it consoles us with the thought that things will be better somewhere, sometime, even if there's not much we can do about it here and now.

Or we can say, if we like, that the reason we have these dreams, the reason we have a sense of a memory of the echo of a voice, is that there is someone speaking to us, whispering in our inner ear—someone who cares very much about this present world and our present selves, and who has made us and the world for a purpose which will indeed involve justice, things being put to rights, *ourselves* being put to rights, the world being rescued at last.

Three of the great religious traditions have taken this last option, and not surprisingly they are related; they are, as it were, second cousins. Judaism speaks of a God who made the world and built into it the passion for justice because it was his own passion. Christianity speaks of this same God having brought that passion into play (indeed, "passion plays" in various senses are a characteristic feature of Christianity) in the life and work of Jesus of Nazareth. Islam draws on some Jewish and some Christian stories and ideas and creates a new synthesis in which the revelation of God's will in the Koran is the ideal which would put the world to rights, if only it were obeyed. There are many differences among these three traditions, but on this point they are agreed, over against other philosophies and religions: the reason we think we have heard a voice is because we have. It wasn't a dream. There are ways of getting back in touch with that voice and making what it says come true. In real life. In *our* real lives.

Tears and Laughter

This book is written to explain and commend one of those traditions, the Christian one. It's about real life, because Christians believe that in Jesus of Nazareth the voice we thought we heard became human and lived and died as one of us. It's about justice, because Christians not only inherit the Jewish passion for justice but claim that Jesus embodied that passion, and that what he did, and what happened to him, set in motion the Creator's plan to rescue the world and put it back to rights. And it is therefore about us, all of us, because we are all involved in this. As we saw, a passion for justice, or at least a sense that things ought to be sorted out, is simply part of being human and living in the world.

You could put it like this. The ancient Greeks told a story of two philosophers. One used to come out of his front door in the morning and roar with laughter. The world was such a comical place that he couldn't help it. The other came out in the morning and burst into tears. The world was so full of sorrow and tragedy that he couldn't help it. In a sense, both were right. Comedy and tragedy both speak of things being out of order—in the one case, simply by being incongruous and therefore funny; in the other case, by things not going the way they should, and people being crushed as a result. Laughter and tears are a good index of being human. Crocodiles look as though they're crying, but they're not sad. You can program a computer to say something funny, but it will never get the joke.

When the early Christians told the story of Jesus—which they did in a number of ways to make a number of different points— they never actually *said* that he laughed, and mentioned only once that he burst into tears. But all the same, the stories they told of him constantly hinted at laughter and tears in fair measure.

Jesus was always going to parties where people had plenty to eat and drink and there seemed to be a celebration going on. He often grossly exaggerated to make his point: here you are, he said, trying to take a speck out of your friend's eye, when you've got a huge great plank in your own eye! He gave his followers, especially the leading ones, funny nicknames ("Peter" means "Rocky"; James and John he called "Thunder-boys"). Wherever he went, people were excited because they believed that God was on the move, that a new rescue operation was in the air, that things were going to be put right. People in that mood are like old friends meeting up at the start of a holiday. They tend to laugh a lot. There is a good time coming. The celebration has begun.

Equally, wherever Jesus went he met an endless supply of people whose lives had gone badly wrong. Sick people, sad people, people in doubt, people in despair, people covering up their uncertainties with arrogant bluster, people using religion as a screen against harsh reality. And though Jesus healed many of them, it wasn't like someone simply waving a magic wand. He shared the pain. He was deeply grieved at the sight of a leper and the thought of all that the man had gone through. He wept at the tomb of a close friend. Toward the end of the story, he himself was in agony, agony of soul before he faced the same agony in his body.

It isn't so much that Jesus laughed *at* the world, or wept *at* the world. He was celebrating *with* the new world that was beginning to be born, the world in which all that was good and lovely would triumph over evil and misery. He was sorrowing *with* the world the way it was, the world of violence and injustice and tragedy which he and the people he met knew so well.

From the very beginning, two thousand years ago, the followers of Jesus have always maintained that he took the tears of the world and made them his own, carrying them all the way to his cruel and unjust death to carry out God's rescue operation; and that he took the joy of the world and brought it to new birth as he rose from the dead and thereby launched God's new creation. That double claim is huge, and I won't even try to explain it until Part Two. But it makes the point that the Christian faith endorses the passion for justice which every human being knows, the longing to see things put to rights. And it claims that in Jesus, God himself has shared this passion and put it into effect, so that in the end all tears may be dried and the world may be filled with justice and joy.

Christians and Justice

"Well," I can hear someone say at this point, "the followers of Jesus haven't made much progress so far, have they? What about the Crusades? What about the Spanish Inquisition? Surely the church has been responsible for more than its own fair share of injustice? What about the people who bomb abortion clinics? What about the fundamentalists who think Armageddon is coming soon so it doesn't matter if they wreck the planet in the meantime? Haven't Christians been part of the problem rather than part of the solution?"

Yes and no.

Yes: from very early on there have always been people who have done terrible things in the name of Jesus. There have also been Christians who have done terrible things knowing them to be terrible things, without claiming that Jesus was supporting them. There's no point hiding from this truth, however uncomfortable it may be.

But also no: because again and again, when we look at the wicked things Christians have done (whether or not they were claiming that God was on their side), we can see in retrospect at least that they were muddled and mistaken about what Christianity actually is. It's no part of Christian belief to say that the followers of Jesus have always got everything right. Jesus himself taught his followers a prayer which includes a clause asking God for forgiveness. He must have thought we would go on needing it.

But at the same time one of the biggest problems with the credibility of the Christian faith in the world today is that a great many people still think of Christianity as identified with "the West" (an odd phrase, since it normally includes Australia and New Zealand, which are about as far east as you can go!)—that is, western Europe and North America in particular, and the cultures which have grown from their earlier colonial settlements. Then, when (as has happened recently) "the West" makes war on some other part of the world, particularly when that part happens to be largely Muslim in religion, it's easy for people to say "the Christians" are making war on "the Muslims." In fact, of course, most people in the Western world are not Christians, and most Christians in today's world do not live in "the West." Most, actually, live in Africa or Southeast Asia. Most "Western" governments do not attempt to put the teaching of Jesus into practice in their societies, and many of them are proud of the fact. But that doesn't stop people putting two and two together and making five—in other words, blaming Christianity for what "the West" chooses to do. The so-called Christian world continues to get bad press, much of it well deserved.

That, actually, is one of the reasons why I have begun this book by talking about justice. It is important to see, and to say, that those who follow Jesus are committed, as he taught us to pray, to God's will being done "on earth as it is in heaven." And that means that God's passion for justice must become ours, too. When Christians use their belief in Jesus as a way of escaping from that demand and challenge, they are abandoning a central element in their own faith. That way danger lies.

Equally, we should not be shy about telling the stories which many skeptics in the Western world have done their best to forget. When the slave trade was at its height, with many people justifying it on the grounds that slaves are mentioned in the Bible, it was a group of devout Christians, led by the unforgettable William Wilberforce in Britain and John Woolman in America, who got together and made it their life's business to stop it. When, with slavery long dead and buried, racial prejudice still haunted the United States, it was the Christian vision of Martin Luther King Jr. that drove him to peaceful, but highly effective, protest. Wilberforce was grasped by a passion for God's justice on behalf of the slaves, a passion which cost him what might otherwise have been a dazzling political career. Martin Luther King's passion for justice for African Americans cost him his life. Their tireless campaigning grew directly and explicitly out of their loyalty to Jesus.

In the same way, when the apartheid regime in South Africa was at its height (with many people justifying it on the grounds that the Bible speaks of different races living different lives), it was the long campaign of Christian leaders like Desmond Tutu that brought about change with remarkably little bloodshed. (I well remember how, in the 1970s, politicians and news commentators took it for granted that change could only come through massive violence.) Tutu and many others did a lot of praying, a lot of reading the Bible with leaders and government officials, a good deal of risky speaking out against the many evil facets of apartheid, and a large amount of equally risky confrontation with black leaders and followers who believed that only violence would work.

Again and again Tutu was caught in the middle, distrusted and hated by both sides. But under the new post-apartheid government he chaired the most extraordinary commission ever to grace the political scene: the South African Commission for Truth and Reconciliation, which has begun the long and painful process of healing the memory and imagination of a whole country, of allowing grief to take its proper course and anger to be expressed and dealt with. Who in the 1960s or even the 1980s would have thought such a thing possible? Yet it happened; and all because of people whose passion for justice and loyalty to Jesus combined to bring it about.

These stories, and many others like them, need to be told and retold. They recount the sort of thing that can and often does happen when people take the Christian message seriously. Sometimes taking it seriously, and speaking out as a result, has gotten people into deep trouble, has even led to a violent death: the twentieth century saw a great many Christians martyred not only for their stance on matters of faith but more especially because their faith led them to fearless action in the cause of justice. Think of Dietrich Bonhoeffer, killed by the Nazis toward the end of the Second World War. Think of Oscar Romero, shot by an assassin because he was speaking out on behalf of the poor in El Salvador. Think, again, of Martin Luther King Jr.

They and nine others are commemorated in statues on the west front of London's Westminster Abbey. They are a reminder to our contemporary world that the Christian faith still makes waves in the world, and that people are prepared to risk their lives out of the passion for justice which it sustains.

That passion, I have been arguing in this chapter, is a central feature of all human life. It is expressed in different ways, and it can sometimes get twisted and go horribly wrong. There are still mobs, and even individuals, who are prepared to kill someone—anyone—in the distorted belief that, as long as someone gets killed, some kind of justice is being done. But all people know, in cooler moments, that this strange thing we call justice, this longing for things to be put right, remains one of the great human goals and dreams. Christians believe that this is so because all humans have heard, deep within themselves, the echo of a voice which calls us to live like that. And they believe that in Jesus that voice became human and did what had to be done to bring it about.

Before we can go any further down that road, we need to listen for other echoes of the same voice. And the first echo we overhear is one which more and more people are listening to these days.

Two

The Hidden Spring

There was once a powerful dictator who ruled his country with an iron will. Every aspect of life was thought through and worked out according to a rational system. Nothing was left to chance.

The dictator noticed that the water sources around the country were erratic and in some cases dangerous. There were thousands of springs of water, often in the middle of towns and cities. They could be useful, but sometimes they caused floods, sometimes they got polluted, and often they burst out in new places and damaged roads, fields, and houses.

The dictator decided on a sensible, rational policy. The whole country, or at least every part where there was any suggestion of water, would be paved over with concrete so thick that no spring of water could ever penetrate it. The water that people needed would be brought to them by a complex system of pipes. Furthermore, the dictator decided, he would use the opportunity, while he was at it, to put into the water various chemicals that would make the people healthy. With the dictator controlling the supply, everyone would have what he decided they needed, and there wouldn't be any more nuisance from unregulated springs.

For many years the plan worked just fine. People got used to their water coming from the new system. It sometimes tasted a bit strange, and from time to time they would look back wistfully to the bubbling streams and fresh springs they used to enjoy. Some of the problems that people had formerly blamed on unregulated water hadn't gone away. It turned out that the air was just as polluted as the water had sometimes been, but the dictator couldn't, or didn't, do much about that. But mostly the new system seemed efficient. People praised the dictator for his forward-looking wisdom.

A generation passed. All seemed to be well. Then, without warning, the springs that had gone on bubbling and sparkling beneath the solid concrete could no longer be contained. In a sudden explosion—a cross between a volcano and an earthquake—they burst through the concrete that people had come to take for granted. Muddy, dirty water shot into the air and rushed through the streets and into houses, shops, and factories. Roads were torn up; whole cities were in chaos. Some people were delighted: at last they could get water again without depending on The System. But the people who ran the official waterpipes were at a loss: suddenly everyone had more than enough water, but it wasn't pure and couldn't be controlled. . . .

We in the Western world are the citizens of that country. The dictator is the philosophy that has shaped our world for the past two or more centuries, making most people materialists by default. And the water is what we today call "spirituality," the hidden spring that bubbles up within human hearts and human societies.

Many people today hear the very word "spirituality" like travelers in a desert hearing news of an oasis. This isn't surprising. The skepticism that we've been taught for the last two hundred years has paved our world with concrete, making people ashamed to admit that they have had profound and powerful "religious" experiences. Where before they would have gone to church, said their prayers, worshipped in this way or that, and understood what they were doing as part of the warp and woof of the rest of life, the mood of the Western world from roughly the 1780s through to the 1980s was very different. We will pipe you (said the prevailing philosophy) the water you need; we will arrange for "religion" to become a small subdepartment of ordinary life; it will be quite safe—harmless, in fact—with church life carefully separated off from everything else in the world, whether politics, art, sex, economics, or whatever. Those who want it can have enough to keep them going. Those who don't want their life, and their way of life, disrupted by anything "religious" can enjoy driving along concrete roads, visiting concrete-based shopping malls, living in concrete-floored houses. Live as if the rumor of God had never existed! We are, after all, in charge of our own fate! We are the captains of our own souls (whatever they may be)! That is the philosophy which has dominated our culture. From this point of view, spirituality is a private hobby, an up-market version of daydreaming for those who like that kind of thing.

Millions in the Western world have enjoyed the temporary separation from "religious" interference that this philosophy has brought. Millions more, aware of the deep subterranean bubblings and yearnings of the water systems we call "spirituality," which can no more ultimately be denied than can endless springs of water under thick concrete, have done their best secretly to tap into it, using the official channels (the churches), but aware that there's more water available than most churches have let on. Many more again have been aware of an indefinable thirst, a longing for springs of living, refreshing water that they can bathe in, delight in, and drink to the full.

Now at last it has happened: the hidden springs have erupted, the concrete foundation has burst open, and life can never be the same again. The official guardians of the old water system (many of whom work in the media and in politics, and some of whom, naturally enough, work in the churches) are of course horrified to see the volcano of "spirituality" that has erupted in recent years. All this "New Age" mysticism, with Tarot cards, crystals, horoscopes, and so on; all this fundamentalism, with militant Christians, militant Sikhs, militant Muslims, and many others bombing each other with God on their side. Surely, say the guardians of the official water system, all this is terribly unhealthy? Surely it will lead us back to superstition, to the old chaotic, polluted, and irrational water supply?

They have a point. But they must face a question in response: Does the fault not lie with those who wanted to pave over the springs with concrete in the first place? September 11, 2001, serves as a reminder of what happens when you try to organize a world on the assumption that religion and spirituality are merely private matters, and that what really matters is economics and politics instead. It wasn't just concrete floors, it was massive towers, that were smashed to pieces that day, by people driven by "religious" beliefs so powerful that the believers were ready to die for them. What should we say? That this merely shows how dangerous "religion" and "spirituality" really are? Or that we should have taken them into account all along?

Thirsty for Spirituality

"The hidden spring" of spirituality is the second feature of human life which, I suggest, functions as the echo of a voice; as a signpost pointing away from the bleak landscape of modern secularism and toward the possibility that we humans are made for more than this. There are many signs that, just as people in eastern Europe are rediscovering freedom and democracy, people in western Europe are rediscovering spirituality—even if some of the experiments in getting back on track are random, haphazard, or even downright dangerous.

This may seem to some a fairly Eurocentric point of view. In much (though not all) of North America, spirituality of one sort or another has never been out of fashion in the same way as it has in Europe. Things are, however, more complicated than that. It has been axiomatic in North America that religion and spirituality should stay in their proper place—in other words, well away from the rest of real life. Just because far more Americans go to church than Europeans, that doesn't mean that the same pressures to stifle the hidden spring have not been operating, or that the same questions haven't been surfacing.

When we look further afield, we quickly realize that, for most parts of the world, the project to pave everything with concrete has never really taken hold. If we think of Africa, the Middle East, the Far East, and for that matter Central and South America—in other words, the great majority of the human race—we find that something we could broadly describe as "spirituality" has been a constant factor in the life of families and villages, towns and cities, communities and societies. It takes different forms. It integrates in a thousand different ways with politics, with music, with art, with drama—in other words, with everyday life.

From our Western perspective, this may appear odd. Anthropologists and other travelers sometimes comment on how quaint it is that people from otherwise sophisticated cultures (Japan, say) still cling to what from our perspective looks like a set of old superstitions. How strange that they still drink from the bubbling springs right at hand, when we've learned how much healthier it is to have our water piped and sanitized by a proper authority. But there are signs all around that we're no longer happy to think like this. We're ready to look again at the springs. Sometimes (from the Christian perspective this often seems funny) newspaper columnists report having visited a church or cathedral, *and having found it moving, and even enjoyable.* Surely, they imply, all right-thinking people had given up that kind of thing? They are usually quick to distance themselves from any suggestion of actually believing in the Christian message. But the sound of fresh bubbling water is hard to ignore. Fewer and fewer people, even in our materialistic world, are even trying to resist it.

This resurgence of interest in a different kind of life to that which can be put into a test tube and measured has taken many different forms. In 1969 the world-famous biologist Sir Alister Hardy founded the Religious Experience Research Unit. He broadcast an appeal for people to write in with stories of their own experience, intending to collect and classify the results in much the same way as nineteenth-century biologists and naturalists had collected and classified data about the myriad forms of life on our planet. The project has grown, and has collected over time a significant archive of material which can now be accessed via the World Wide Web (http://www.archiveshub.ac.uk/news/ahrerca.html). Anyone who supposes that religious experience is a minority interest, or that it has been steadily dying out as people in the modern world become more sophisticated, should look at the material and think again.

You would get a similar result if you went into a bookstore and looked at the section on spirituality. Actually, one of the signs of the times is that bookstores don't know what to call this category. Sometimes it's labeled "Spirituality" or "Mind, Body, and Spirit." Sometimes it's called "Religion"—though normally that leads you to leather-bound Bibles and prayer books designed to be given as presents, not to offer you springs of living water. Sometimes it's called "Self-Help," as though spirituality were some kind of do-it-yourself project, a weekend activity to make you feel better about yourself.

What you find in such sections is typically a rich mixture, depending on the manager and style of the bookstore. Sometimes there are some quite serious works of theology. Usually there are books to help you discover your "personality type" on one of the popular systems—the Myers-Briggs Type Indicator, for instance, or the Enneagram. Sometimes we are enticed further afield—into (for instance) exploring reincarnation: perhaps, if we discover who we were in a former life, we will understand why we think and feel the way we do now. Alternatively, many writers have urged us toward a kind of nature-mysticism in which we get in touch with the deep cycles and rhythms of the world around us, and indeed within us. Sometimes the movement is the other way, suggesting a quasi-Buddhist detachment from the world, a withdrawal into a spiritual world where the outward things of life cease to be so important. Sometimes a sudden fad sweeps across the Western world, whether for Kabbalah (originally a type of medieval Jewish mysticism, now subverted in some quarters into mere postmodern mumbo jumbo), for labyrinths (aids to prayer in some medieval cathedrals, notably Chartres, now more widely used in a blend of Christian spirituality and late-modern self-discovery), or for pilgrimage, where spiritual hunger rubs shoulders with globe-trotting curiosity.

In particular, and related especially to the part of the world where I now live—Great Britain—the last generation has seen a sudden upsurge of interest in all things Celtic. Indeed, the very word "Celtic" is enough, when attached to music, prayers, buildings, jewelry, T-shirts, and anything else that comes to hand, to win the attention, and often enough the money, of people in today's Western culture. It seems to speak of a haunting possibility of another world, a world in which God (whoever he may be) is more directly present, a world in which humans get along better with their natural environment, a world with roots far deeper, and a hidden music far richer, than the shrill and shallow world of modern technology, soap operas, and football managers. The world of the ancient Celts—Northumbria, Wales, Cornwall, Brittany, Ireland, and Scotland—seems a million miles from modern-day Christianity. That is, no doubt, why it is so attractive to people bored or even angry with official religion in Western churches.

But the real center of Celtic Christianity—the monastic life, with great stress on extreme bodily asceticism and energetic evangelism—is hardly what people are looking for today. St. Cuthbert, one of the greatest of the Celtic saints, used to pray standing up to his waist in the sea off the northeast coast of England. There's no evidence that the sea there was any less bitterly cold then than it is in our own day. Nor are there signs of today's cheerful Celtic enthusiasts embracing that kind of mortification of the flesh.

Rich and deep experiences of the type we call "spiritual" often—indeed, normally—engage the emotions in very profound ways. Sometimes such experiences produce such a deep sense of inner peace and happiness that people speak of having been for a while in

what they can only call "heaven." Sometimes they even laugh out
loud for sheer happiness. Sometimes the experience is of a sharing
in the suffering of the world which is so painful and raw that the
only possible response is to weep bitterly. I am not talking about
the sense of well-being, or its opposite, that might come as a result
of engaging in some deeply satisfying activity on the one hand, or
in confronting some awful tragedy on the other. I am speaking of
those widely reported times in which people have had the sense of
living for a while in multiple dimensions not normally accessible
to us, in one of which they experienced either such a wonderful
resolution and joy, or such anguish and torment, as to make them
react as though they were really undergoing those things for themselves. Such experiences, as every seasoned pastor or spiritual guide
knows, can have a lasting and profound effect on one's life.

So what are we to make of "spirituality" as we listen for the
echoes of a voice that might be addressing us?

What Makes Us So Thirsty?

The Christian explanation of the renewed interest in spirituality is quite straightforward. If anything like the Christian story is
in fact true (in other words, if there is a God whom we can know
most clearly in Jesus), this interest is exactly what we should expect;
because in Jesus we glimpse a God who loves people and wants
them to know and respond to that love. In fact, this is what we
should expect if *any* of the stories told by religious people—that
is, the great majority of people who have ever lived—are true: if
there is any kind of divine force or being, it is at least thinkable that
humans would find some kind of engagement with this being or
power to be an attractive or at least interesting phenomenon.

This is precisely why there are such things as religions in the first
place. When the astronomers see that a planet is behaving in a way
they can't explain by reference to other already known planets, or
to the sun itself, they postulate a further planet of a sort, size, and

location that will explain the strange behavior. That's actually how the remoter planets were discovered. When physicists discover phenomena they can explain by no other means, they postulate new entities, not themselves capable of being directly observed, which explain them. That's how quarks and similar strange things have entered our language and understanding.

On the other hand, part of the Christian story (and for that matter, the Jewish and Muslim stories) is that human beings have been so seriously damaged by evil that what they need isn't simply better self-knowledge, or better social conditions, but help, and indeed rescue, from outside themselves. We should expect that in the quest for spiritual life many people will embrace options that are, to put it no more strongly for the moment, less than what would actually be best for them. People who have been starved of water for a long time will drink anything, even if it is polluted. People kept without food for long periods will eat anything they can find, from grass to uncooked meat. Thus by itself "spirituality" may appear to be part of the problem as well as part of the solution.

There are, of course, other ways of explaining both the hunger for spirituality and the strange things people sometimes do to satisfy it. Many people at various stages of history, the last two hundred years in the Western world being one such time, have offered alternative accounts of this sense of a shared spiritual quest. "The fool says in his heart, 'There is no God'"—that was the verdict of an ancient Israelite poet (Psalm 14:1 and elsewhere)—yet there are many who have declared that it is the believer who is the fool. Spirituality is all the result of psychological forces, said Freud, such as projecting memories of a father-figure onto a cosmic screen. It's all imagination or wishful thinking or both. The fact that people are hungry for spirituality doesn't *prove* anything. If the call to spirituality that we hear can be interpreted as the echo of a voice, it's one which is lost in the wind as quickly as it comes, leaving us to ask ourselves whether we imagined it or whether, if we really did hear something, it was simply the echo of our own voices.

But the question of why we yearn for spirituality is worth asking nonetheless. After all, if the contemporary quest for spirituality is based on the idea that there's someone or something "out there" with whom (or with which) we can be in contact, and if that idea is after all completely mistaken (so that we humans are in that sense alone in the cosmos), then spirituality might not be simply a harmless pursuit. It might actually be dangerous, if not to ourselves, then at least to those whose lives are affected by what we say and do. Some hard-nosed skeptics, seeing the damage done by (what they would call) religious fanatics—suicide bombers, apocalyptic fantasists, and the like—have declared that the sooner we recognize all this religion as a kind of neurosis, and either pay it no further attention or even try to have it banned outright or confined to the safety of consenting adults in private, the better. Every so often one hears on the radio, or reads in the newspaper, that some scientist has claimed to find the neuron, or even the gene, which controls what seem (to the subject) to be "religious" experiences, with the result that such experiences are declared to be nothing more than internal mental or emotional events. Experiences like that, however powerful, would be no more of a signpost to an external reality than my toothache would be a sign that someone had punched me on the jaw. It is difficult to demonstrate, especially to a confirmed skeptic, that my spiritual experiences have any purchase on external reality.

Spirituality and Truth

One of the regular tactics the skeptic employs at this point is relativism. I vividly remember a school friend saying to me in exasperation, at the end of a conversation about Christian faith, "It's obviously true for you, but that doesn't mean it's true for anybody else." Many people today take exactly that line.

Saying "It's true for you" sounds fine and tolerant. But it only works because it's twisting the word "true" to mean, not "a true revelation of the way things are in the real world," but "something that is genuinely happening inside you." In fact, saying "It's true for you" in this sense is more or less equivalent to saying "It's *not* true for you," because the "it" in question—the spiritual sense or awareness or experience—is conveying, very powerfully, a message (that there is a loving God) which the challenger is reducing to something else (that you are having strong feelings which you misinterpret in that sense). This goes with several other pressures which have combined to make the notion of "truth" itself highly problematic within our world.

Once we see that the skeptic's retort is itself open to problems of this sort, we return to the possibility that the widespread hunger for spirituality, which has been reported in various ways across the whole of human experience, is a genuine signpost to something which remains just around the corner, out of sight. It may be the echo of a voice—a voice which is calling, not so loudly as to compel us to listen whether we choose to or not, but not so quietly as to be drowned out altogether by the noises going on in our heads and our world. If it were to join itself up with the passion for justice, some might conclude that it would at least be worth listening for further echoes of the same voice.

†

Three

Made for Each Other

We were made for each other."
The young couple gazed into each other's eyes as they sat on the sofa in my study. They had come to arrange their wedding: full of dreams and wonder at discovering such perfection in another person, someone so exactly what they were looking and hoping for.

And yet, as we all know, marriages apparently made in heaven sometimes end not far from hell. Although to couples in the first flush of romance the very thought of each other adds a whole glorious new dimension to their lives, statistics suggest that, unless they know how to navigate the road that lies ahead, they may soon be yelling and sobbing and calling the divorce lawyers.

Isn't there something odd about this? How is it that we ache for each other and yet find relationships so difficult? My proposal is that the whole area of human relationships forms another "echo of a voice"—an echo which we can ignore if we choose to do so, but which is loud enough to get through the defenses of a good many people within the supposedly modern secular world. Or, if you prefer, human relationships are another signpost pointing away into a mist, telling us that there is a road ahead which leads to . . . well, which leads somewhere we might want to go.

I begin with the romantic relationship because, despite all the debunking of marriage in Western culture over the last generation, despite the desire for independence, the pressures on double-career couples, the soaring divorce rates, and a world full of new temptations, marriage is still remarkably popular. Millions, perhaps billions, of dollars are spent on weddings every year. And yet every other play, film, and novel, and perhaps one in ten newspaper reports, involves domestic tragedy—which is a fancy way of saying that something went dramatically wrong with a central relationship, usually that between a married couple.

We are made for each other. Yet making relationships work, let alone making them flourish, is often remarkably difficult. That is the same paradox that we uncovered in the previous two chapters. We all know that justice matters, yet it slips through our fingers. We mostly know that there is such a thing as spirituality, and that it's important, yet it's hard to refute the charge that it's all wishful thinking. In the same way, we all know that we belong in communities, that we were made to be social creatures. Yet there are many times when we are tempted to slam the door and stomp off into the night by ourselves, simultaneously making the statement that we don't belong anymore and that we want someone to take pity on us, to come to the rescue and comfort us. We all know we belong in relationships, but we can't quite work out how to get them right. The voice we hear echoing in our heads and our hearts keeps reminding us of both parts of this paradox, and it's worth pondering why.

The Puzzle of Relationships

Of course, being by yourself is often very desirable. If you work in a noisy factory, or even if you live in a crowded home, getting away, perhaps out into the countryside, can be a blessed relief. Even those of us who like being with lots of other people can sometimes have enough of it and enjoy curling up with a book, or going for a long walk and thinking about things without other voices intruding. Differences of temperament, upbringing, and other circumstances have a large part to play in this.

But most people don't want complete, long-term solitariness. In fact, most people, even those who are naturally shy and introverted, don't normally choose to be alone all the time. Of those who opt for a solitary life, some do so for religious reasons, becoming hermits. Others do so to escape danger, as when a convicted criminal chooses solitary confinement rather than face prison violence. But even those who make such choices are usually conscious that what they're doing is abnormal. Indeed, sometimes when people are locked up by themselves they quite literally go mad. Without human society, they don't know who they are anymore. It seems that we humans were designed to find our purpose and meaning not simply in ourselves and our own inner lives, but in one another and in the shared meanings and purposes of a family, a street, a workplace, a community, a town, a nation. When we describe someone as a "loner," we're not necessarily saying the person is bad, simply that he or she is unusual.

Relationships come in different shapes. One of the oddities about the modern Western world is the remolding (and shrinking) of relationships that we have come to take for granted. Anyone growing up in an average African town has dozens of friends up and down the street; indeed, many children live within what to Western eyes would look like a massive and confusing extended family, with virtually every adult within walking distance being treated as an honorary aunt or uncle in a way that is unimaginable in the modern West. In such a community, there exist multiple networks of support, encouragement, rebuke, and warning, a corporate repository of folk wisdom (or, as it might be, folk folly) which keeps everyone together and gives people a shared sense of direction or at least, when things are bad, a shared sense of misfortune. Those who live in today's Western world mostly don't even realize what they're missing. In fact, they might be alarmed at the thought of all that togetherness. In such a community, everyone is in it together, for good or ill.

And sometimes, of course, it is indeed for ill. A strong sense of corporate solidarity can condition an entire community to go rushing off in the wrong direction. Times when communities have been most united, when people have pulled most solidly together, have included times when, for instance, the population of ancient Athens voted arrogantly for wars they couldn't win. More recently, they included the time when the great majority of the German people voted to give Adolf Hitler an absolute power that changed the course of history. Even when communities are functioning well in terms of their own inner dynamics, there is no guarantee that the results will be healthy.

And of course many communities find it hard to work well together in the first place. If the struggles of modern marriages are one obvious example, another is the fragile state of our contemporary democracies. Most people in today's Western world can't envision living in any kind of state other than a democratic one, and would certainly not choose to do so. The very word "democracy," carrying at least the meaning of "full adult voting rights" (as against, say, systems in which women or the poor or slaves are excluded—systems which have been common in the past, and have called themselves "democracies"), has come to carry the highest approval rating possible. If you say you don't believe in democracy, or even that you question aspects of it, people treat you as if you're mad, or at least highly dangerous.

But there are signs that all is not well with democracy, at least as we have known it. We cannot get our relationships right at the large level any more than at the small. In the United States, for example, it is taken for granted that if you wish to run for major office, let alone for the presidency, you need to have lots of money, much of it probably raised from very rich backers. But people do not lightly part with large sums of money; supporters routinely look for some kind of payback, not least as the price of continuing support next time around. The more people see this going on, the more it generates cynicism; and cynicism gnaws away at the heart of our national and civic relationships. In Britain, more people now vote on "reality TV" shows (voting, for instance, to eject a contestant from a "Big

Brother" house) than vote in elections. I'm talking about general elections here—choosing a government for the whole country for up to five years—not local elections, where the turnout is usually much lower still. And when, as has happened many times in recent decades, the party that "wins" the election turns out to have garnered only a paltry fraction of all the votes cast, serious questions are raised about the system as a whole. In many Western countries there's similar dissatisfaction with the way things are operating. We all know we belong together in some sense or other, but it's not at all clear how that can or should work.

Thus from the most intimate relationship (marriage) to those on the largest scale (national institutions) we find the same thing: we all know we are made to live together, but we all find that doing so is more difficult than we had imagined. And it is within these settings, large and small, but particularly at the more personal and intimate end of the scale, that we find the natural setting of those characteristic signs of human life: laughter and tears. We find each other funny. We find each other tragic. We find *ourselves,* and our relationships, funny and tragic. This is who we are. We can't avoid being this way, and we don't want to, even though things often don't work out the way we want.

Confusion About Sex

At the heart of relationships we find sex. Not, of course, that all relationships are sexual in the sense of involving erotic behavior. Virtually all societies treat such behavior as something to be contained in certain very specific contexts, often within marriage or close equivalents. And yet when human beings relate to one another, they relate as male and female; maleness and femaleness are not identities which we only assume when we enter into one particular kind of relationship (namely, a romantic or erotic one). Here, too, we all know in our bones that we are a particular kind of creature, and yet that we find it difficult to handle *being* this kind of creature. Sex is, in other words, a particularly sharp example of the paradox I am high-lighting. It may seem, in today's world, an unlikely location to catch the echoes of a voice of the sort that I have been describing. That, however, only shows how badly we have misunderstood things.

Recent generations in the West have seen huge efforts expended on the attempt to teach boys and girls that the differences between them are simply a matter of biological function. We have been sternly warned against stereotyping people according to their gender. More and more jobs have become, at least in theory, inter-changeable between genders. And yet today's parents, however impeccable their idealistic credentials, have discovered that most little boys like playing with toy guns and cars, and that a remark-able number of little girls like playing with dolls, dressing them up and nursing them. Nor is it only children who stubbornly resist the new rules. Those who target magazines at different groups in soci-ety have no difficulty in producing "men's magazines" that very few women would buy, and "women's magazines" that hardly any men would read. The circulation of such magazines goes from strength to strength, even in those countries where the propaganda about gender identity has been strong for decades. In most countries, of course, nobody bothers to try to pretend that men and women are identical and interchangeable. Everyone knows that they are remarkably different.

It is, however, harder than normally imagined to plot exact-ly what these differences are, not least because different societies have different images of what men should do and what women should do, and are then puzzled when not everyone conforms to type. I am not at all denying that there are many areas where we have gotten this wrong in the past. I have argued strenu-ously in my own sphere of work for far more interchangeabili-ty than has traditionally been the case. My point is simply this: that all human relationships involve an element of gender iden-tity (I, as a man, relate to other men as man to man, to women as man to woman), and that though we all know this deep down, we become remarkably confused about it. At one end of the scale, some people try to pretend that for all practical purposes their gender is irrelevant, as though they were in fact neuter. At the other end, some people are always sizing others up as potential sexual partners, even if only in imagination. And, again, we know in our bones that both of these are distortions of reality.

Both responses, in fact, involve a form of denial. The former (imaging ourselves to be neuter) involves denying something deeply important about who we are and how we are made. We simply *are* gendered beings; and since this affects all kinds of attitudes and reactions, in numerous and subtle ways, we gain nothing by pretending that we're not and that it doesn't. The latter response (seeing other people as potential sexual partners) involves denying something hugely important about the nature of erotic relationships—namely, that there is no such thing as "casual sex." Just as sexual identity—maleness and femaleness—goes near the heart of who we are as human beings, so sexual activity burns a pathway into the core of our human identity and self-awareness. To deny this, whether in theory or in action, is to collude with the dehumanization of our relationships, to embrace a living death. In short, we all know that sex and gender are hugely important to human living. But in this area we discover something that's true of *all* aspects of human relationship: that things are far more complicated than we might have imagined, far more fraught with difficulty, puzzles, and paradoxes.

Sex and death, in fact, seem to have a lot to do with one another, and not only in second-rate novels and movies. And it is death that seems to call into question the very notion that we are made for relationship at all.

Death—and the Call to Genuine Humanness

We search for justice, but we often find that it eludes us. We hunger for spirituality, but we often live as though one-dimensional materialism were the obvious truth. In the same way, the finest and best of our relationships will eventually end in death. The laughter will end in tears. We know it; we fear it; but there's nothing we can do about it.

If this is paradoxical—we're meant for relationship, but all relationships come to an end—we find in both parts an echoing voice that reminds us of the echoes we have heard in the first two chapters. Those faith-systems which are rooted in the scriptures we call the Old Testament speak of human beings as made, irreducibly, for relationship: for relationship with one another within the human family (and especially within the male-female complementarity); for relationship with the rest of the created order; and for relationship, above all, with the Creator. And yet, within the story of creation which remains foundational for Judaism, Christianity, and Islam, all things within the present world are transient. They are not designed to be permanent.

That impermanence—the fact of death, in other words—has now attained the dark note of tragedy. It is bound up with human rebellion against the Creator, with a rejection of that deepest of relationships and a consequent souring of the other two (with one another and with the created order). But the motifs of relationship and impermanence are part of the very structure of what, in the great monotheistic religions, it means to be human. We shouldn't be surprised that, when we think of human relationships, we find ourselves hearing the echo of a voice, even if, as in Genesis, the voice is asking "Where are you?"

The ancient biblical creation story offers a powerful and pregnant picture for all this: humans, it says, are made in God's image. At first sight, that doesn't help much, since we don't know very much about God and thus can't deduce very much about who we are supposed to be. Nor (it seems) do we know as much as we might like about who we are, and so we can't deduce very much about God either. But the point being made in Genesis is probably a different one. In the ancient world, as indeed in some parts of the modern one, great rulers would often set up statues of themselves in prominent places, not so much in their own home territory (where everyone knew who they were and recognized that they were in charge), but in their foreign or far-flung dominions. Far more statues of Roman emperors, for example, were found in Greece, Turkey, and Egypt than in Italy or Rome itself. For an emperor, the point of placing an image of yourself in the subject territory was that the subjects in that country would be reminded that you were their ruler, and would conduct themselves accordingly.

That has, to us, a threatening sound. We are democrats, after all. We don't want far-off rulers giving us orders, still less (as we rightly suspect) demanding our money. But that only shows how much our relationships—with God, with the world, and with one another—have been flawed and corrupted. In the early stories, the point was that the Creator loved the world he had made, and wanted to look after it in the best possible way. To that end, he placed within his world a looking-after creature, a creature who would demonstrate to the creation who he, the Creator, really was, and who would set to work developing the creation and making it flourish and fulfill its purpose. This looking-after creature (or rather, this family of creatures: the human race) would model and embody that interrelatedness, that mutual and fruitful knowing, trusting and loving, which was the Creator's intention. Relationship was part of the way in which we were meant to be fully human, not for our own sake, but as part of a much larger scheme of things. And our failures in human relationship are thereby woven into our failures in the other large projects of which we know in our bones that we are part: our failure to put the world to rights in systems of justice (Chapter One), and our failure to maintain and develop that spirituality which, at its heart, involves a relationship of trust and love with the Creator (Chapter Two).

But the failures themselves, and the fact that we know of them in our bones, point to something which only the Christian tradition, out of the great monotheistic faiths, has explored in any detail: the belief that the Creator himself contains, within himself, a multiple relationship. This is something we will examine later on. But it indicates well enough that if, as I have suggested here, we do indeed know that we are made for relationships and that we find relationships difficult, we can see this double knowledge as a further signpost pointing in the same direction as the two we have already examined. The call to relationship, and the sad rebuke for our failures at it, can be heard together as echoes of a voice. The voice is reminding us of who we really are. It may even be offering us some kind of rescue from our predicament.

We can already tell enough about that voice that we would know its owner if we met it. Its owner would be one who was totally committed to relationships of every sort—with other human beings, with the Creator, with the natural world. And yet that owner would share the pain of the brokenness of each of these relationships. One of the central elements of the Christian story is the claim that the paradox of laughter and tears, woven as it is deep into the heart of all human experience, is woven also deep into the heart of God.

✝

Four

For the Beauty of
the Earth

One day, rummaging through a dusty old attic in a small Austrian town, a collector comes across a faded manuscript containing many pages of music. It is written for the piano. Curious, he takes it to a dealer. The dealer phones a friend, who appears half an hour later. When he sees the music he becomes excited, then puzzled. This looks like the handwriting of Mozart himself, but it isn't a well-known piece. In fact, he's never heard it. More phone calls. More excitement. More consultations. It really does seem to be Mozart. And, though some parts seem distantly familiar, it doesn't correspond to anything already known in his works.

Before long, someone is sitting at a piano. The collector stands close by, not wanting to see his precious find damaged as the pianist turns the pages. But then comes a fresh surprise. The music is wonderful. It's just the sort of thing Mozart would have written. It's energetic and elegiac by turns; it's got subtle harmonic shifts, some splendid tunes, and a ringing finale. But it seems . . . incomplete. There are places where nothing much seems to be happening, where the piano is simply marking time. There are other places where the writing is faded and it isn't quite clear, but it *looks* as though the composer has indicated, not just one or two bars rest, but a much longer pause.

Gradually the truth dawns on the excited little group. What they are looking at is indeed by Mozart. It is indeed beautiful. But it's the piano part of a piece that involves another instrument, or perhaps other instruments. By itself it is frustratingly incomplete. A further search of the attic reveals nothing else that would provide a clue. The piano music is all there is, a signpost to something that was there once and might still turn up one day. There must have been a complete work of art which would now, without additional sheet music, be almost impossible to reconstruct; they don't know if the piano was to accompany an oboe or a bassoon, a violin or a cello, or perhaps a full string quartet or some other combination of instruments. If those other parts could be found, they would make complete sense of the incomplete beauty contained in the faded scribble of genius now before them.

(In case anyone should wonder, by the way, I wrote these paragraphs some months before a librarian in Philadelphia came upon a Beethoven manuscript which turned out to be the composer's own transcription, for two pianos, of the "Great Fugue" from one of his final string quartets. Life and art have an odd habit of dancing together in multiple mutual imitation.)

This is the position we are in when confronted by beauty. The world is full of beauty, but the beauty is incomplete. Our puzzlement about what beauty is, what it means, and what (if anything) it is there *for* is the inevitable result of looking at one part of a larger whole. Beauty, in other words, is another echo of a voice—a voice which (from the evidence before us) might be saying one of several different things, but which, were we to hear it in all its fullness, would make sense of what we presently see and hear and know and love and call "beautiful."

The Transience of Beauty

Beauty, like justice, slips through our fingers. We photograph the sunset, but all we get is the memory of the moment, not the moment itself. We buy the recording, but the symphony says something different when we listen to it at home. We climb the mountain, and though the view from the summit is indeed magnificent, it leaves us wanting more; even if we could build a house there and gaze all day at the scene, the itch wouldn't go away. Indeed, the beauty sometimes seems to be in the itching itself, the sense of longing, the kind of pleasure which is exquisite and yet leaves us unsatisfied.

Actually, that last phrase—exquisite, yet leaving us unsatisfied—is what Oscar Wilde said about a cigarette. And that shows something else about the way in which beauty presents us with a haunting paradox. Few today, faced with the statistics about lung cancer, would give such high aesthetic standing to a cigarette (even if, as so often with Wilde, the *bon mot* was designed to shock in the first place). But tastes and fashions change, in beauty as in many other things. They change so thoroughly that we are forced to ask whether beauty is after all simply in the eye of the beholder, or whether we can give any more satisfactory account of it which will leave us—like the frustrated but excited music collectors—in possession of one part at least of the complete whole.

I think of this puzzle whenever I see, from another time and place, a picture of a woman whose contemporaries obviously thought her extremely beautiful. Look at the paintings on Greek vases, or on the walls of Pompeii. Look at the Egyptian portraits of great, noble women whose beauty was obviously highly prized. Look, even, at some of the portraits from three or four hundred years ago, and see what people of their day said about them. Frankly, I wouldn't turn my head in the street to gaze at any of them. Helen of Troy may have had a face that, in her day, launched a thousand ships, but most of us now wouldn't rate her as worth a single rowboat.

The same is true of the beauty of nature. For the last two hundred years, and especially since Wordsworth and the Lakeland poets, most people have regarded the wild scenery of the English Lake

District as spectacularly beautiful, evocative, and powerful. Scene after scene has been painted times without number. Many Britons who have never been near the Lake District possess placemats displaying the Langdale Pikes, or the view of Skiddaw with the town of Keswick nestling at its foot—just as, in America, many possess prints of Ansel Adams displaying the glories of Yosemite. And yet in earlier days mountainous scenery wasn't seen as beautiful and evocative, but as fearsome, dark, and dangerous. How is it that fashions change so easily?

This is only partially explained by changes in perspective. We admire the grace and power of an Alpine avalanche in a faraway glacier, but our mood changes rapidly if we see a village lying helpless in its path. We stand mesmerized watching ocean waves roll in to shore, each one a miracle of smooth curves and crashing power; but enjoyment turns to horror before the nightmare of a tsunami.

A matter of perspective, then, and a matter of taste, in complex combination. And taste, in addition, changes not just from generation to generation but from person to person and subculture to subculture in the same period, the same town, the same house. The newlyweds discover that the picture he wants to hang above the fireplace appears to her nothing more than sentimental kitsch. The teacher for whom the geometric proof possesses an almost transcendent elegance discovers that, to the class, it is nothing but numbers, lines, and angles.

And how is it that beauty fades so quickly? The glorious sunset is soon over. The young person whose youthful bloom gains admiring glances prolongs his or her good looks for a time with care and a little help from makeup artists, but we know what's coming. Even if we mature in our appreciation of human beauty and learn to love the wise and kindly look in old eyes, and the thousand lines that speak of love and grief and joy and courage, the further we go down that road the closer we are once more to the paradox of the sunset.

Beauty and Truth

"Beauty is truth, truth beauty," wrote Keats; but the puzzles we have glimpsed should prevent us from making such an easy equation. The beauty we know and love is, at best, one part of truth, and not always the most important part. In fact, to identify beauty and truth, in the light of the previous paragraphs, would be to take a large step toward what we now think of as the postmodern dilemma: the collapse of "truth" altogether. If beauty and truth are one and the same, then truth is different for everyone, for every age, and indeed for the same person from year to year. If beauty were hidden in the beholder's eye, then "truth" would be merely a way of talking about the inner feelings that went along with it. And that simply isn't how we normally use the word "truth."

What we must also rule out, along with any identification of beauty and truth, is the idea that beauty gives us direct access to God, to "the divine," or to a transcendent realm of any sort. The fact that the music is clearly designed to go within a larger whole gives us no direct clue as to what that larger whole might be. If, without previous zoological knowledge, you came face-to-face with a male tiger in prime condition, you might be tempted to fall down and worship such a glorious example of form, color, grace, and power. Few examples of idolatry would be so swiftly self-refuting. Beauty is more complicated than that. The paradoxes we have noted tell heavily against the facile identification between God and the natural world to which some generations have been drawn. The beauty of the natural world is, at best, the echo of a voice, not the voice itself. And if we try to pin it down—literally, in the case of a butterfly-collector with a specimen—we find that the key thing itself, the elusive beauty which keeps us always looking further, is precisely what you lose when the pin goes in. Beauty is here, but it's not here. It is this—this bird, this song, this sunset—but it is not this.

Any account of beauty, and especially one which suggests that beauty is a signpost pointing beyond itself, must take account, then, of the two things about it which we have described. On the one hand, we must acknowledge that beauty, whether in the natural order or within human creation, is sometimes so powerful that it evokes our very deepest feelings of awe, wonder, gratitude, and reverence. Almost all humans sense this some of the time at least, even though they disagree wildly about which things evoke which feelings and why. On the other hand, we must acknowledge that these disagreements and puzzles are enough to press some, without an obvious desire to be cynical or destructive, to say that beauty is all in the mind, or the imagination, or the genes. Some will suggest that it's all a matter of evolutionary conditioning: you only like that particular scenery *because* your distant ancestors knew they could find food there. Others may hint at unconscious sexual feelings: Why do little boys like watching trains charge into tunnels? Still others might quite reasonably suggest that it's all about vicarious pleasure: we would like to be among the guests at the dinner party in the painting. It seems we have to hold the two together: beauty is *both* something that calls us out of ourselves *and* something which appeals to feelings deep within us.

At this point some philosophers, going back (as so much does) to Plato, have drawn the two sides together. They suggest that the natural world on the one hand, and the representations of the natural world offered by artists on the other, are reflections of a higher world, a world beyond space, time, and (especially) matter. This world, which Plato called the world of "the Forms" (or Ideas), is, according to the theory, the ultimate reality. Everything in the present world is a copy or shadow of something in that world. This means that everything in our world is indeed a pointer to something in a world beyond, a world which we can learn to contemplate and even to love for its own sake. If we don't make this transition, if we simply accept natural and man-made beauty on its own terms, we mustn't be surprised if it seems, on closer inspection, to collapse into our own subjective feelings. Beauty points away from the present world to a different one altogether.

This suggestion is attractive—at one level. It does indeed make sense of a good part of our experience. But for the three great monotheistic religions at least (or most mainstream versions of them) it gives away far too much. It's all very well to say that beauty in this present world is puzzling, transient, and sometimes apparently only skin deep, while underneath all is worms and rottenness. But if we push that just an inch further, we find ourselves saying that the present world of space, time, and matter is bad *in itself.* If it's a signpost, it's made of wood that's already rotting. If it is a voice, it is the voice of a desperately sick man telling us of the land of health to which he is unable to travel. And this is deeply untrue to the great traditions of Judaism, Christianity, and Islam. The great monotheistic faiths declare, in full view of the apparently contrary evidence, that the present world of space, time, and matter always was and still is the good creation of a good God.

It is also deeply untrue to the experience of humans in every culture and time known to us. Just at the point where we might be ready to give in and admit that it was all a delusion, all in the mind, all explicable in terms of our instincts and genetic makeup, we turn the corner, glimpse the distant hills, smell the new-mown hay, hear the song of a bird . . . and declare, like Dr. Johnson kicking the stone, that it is real, it is outside us, it isn't just imagination. Heaven and earth are full of glory, a glory which stubbornly refuses to be reduced to terms of the senses of the humans who perceive it.

Beauty and God

But whose glory is it?

The Christian tradition has said, and indeed sung, that the glory belongs to God the creator. It is his voice we hear echoing off the crags, murmuring in the sunset. It is his power we feel in the crashing of the waves and the roar of the lion. It is his beauty we see reflected in a thousand faces and forms.

And when the cynic reminds us that people fall off crags, get lost after sunset, and are drowned by waves and eaten by lions; when the cynic cautions that faces get old and lined and forms get pudgy and sick—then we Christians do not declare that it was all a mistake. We do not avail ourselves of Plato's safety hatch and say that the *real* world is not a thing of space, time, and matter but another world into which we can escape. We say that the present world is the real one, and that it's in bad shape but expecting to be repaired. We tell, in other words, the story we told in the first chapter: the story of a good Creator longing to put the world back into the good order for which it was designed. We tell the story of a God who does the two things which, some of the time at least, we know we all want and need: a God who completes what he has begun, a God who comes to the rescue of those who seem lost and enslaved in the world the way it now is.

The idea of God coming to the rescue on the one hand, and of God completing creation and putting it to rights on the other, is highlighted in the book that bears the name of one of the greatest ancient Israelite prophets: Isaiah. In his eleventh chapter the prophet paints a picture of a world put to rights, of the wolf lying down with the lamb, and of the earth being filled with God's glory as the waters cover the sea. This haunting picture is all the more strange because, five chapters earlier, the prophet had told of seeing angels singing that the whole earth was full of God's glory. As a matter of logic, we want to press the writer: Is the earth *already* full of that glory, or is this something which will only happen in the future? As a matter of understanding beauty, we want to ask: Is the beauty we see at the moment complete, or is it incomplete, pointing to something in the future? And as a matter of far more urgent inquiry, we want to ask the writer, perhaps shaking him by the scruff of the neck: If the earth is full of God's glory, why is it also so full of pain and anguish and screaming and despair?

The prophet (or whoever edited his book into the form we now have) has answers for all these questions, but not the sort of answers you can write on the back of a postcard. Nor can we explore them just yet. What we must notice at this stage is that, both in the Old Testament and in the New, the present suffering of the world—about which the biblical writers knew every bit as much as we do—never makes them falter in their claim that the created world really is the good creation of a good God. They live with the tension. And they don't do it by imagining that the present created order is a shabby, second-rate kind of thing, perhaps (as in some kinds of Platonism) made by a shabby, second-rate sort of god. They do it by telling a story of what the one creator God has been doing to rescue his beautiful world and to put it to rights. And the story they tell, which we shall explore further in due course, indicates that the present world really is a signpost to a larger beauty, a deeper truth. It really is the authentic manuscript of one part of a masterpiece. The question is, What is the whole masterpiece like, and how can we begin to hear the music in the way it was intended?

The point of the story is that the masterpiece already exists—in the mind of the composer. At the moment, neither the instruments nor the players are ready to perform it. But when they are, the manuscript we already have—the present world with all its beauty and all its puzzlement—will turn out to be truly part of it. The deficiencies in the one part we possess will be made good. The things that don't make sense at the moment will display a harmony and perfection we hadn't dreamed of. The points at which today the music seems almost perfect, lacking just one small thing, will be completed. That is the promise held out in the story. Just as, in one of the New Testament's greatest claims, the kingdoms of this world are to become the kingdom of God, so the beauty of this world will be enfolded in the beauty of God—and not just the beauty of God himself, but the beauty which, because God is the creator *par excellence,* he will create when the present world is rescued, healed, restored, and completed.

The Glorious Complexity of Life

I gave a lecture not long ago in which I spoke, as I've now done, about justice, spirituality, relationship, and beauty. One of the first questioners afterward asked me why I hadn't given equal air time to truth. It's a fair question. In a sense the question of truth has haunted the whole discussion so far, and will continue to do so.

The questions, What is true? and How do we know? have been central to most major philosophies. And they force us back to deeper questions, the annoying ones which thinkers always insist on asking: What do you mean by "true," and, for that matter, what do you mean by "know"? What I have done so far in this book is to take four issues that might, for most humans in most cultures, raise questions and point to unrealized possibilities. These are things which might well function, across all types of human society, as signposts to something which matters a great deal but which we can't grasp in the way we grasp the distance from London to New York, or the right way to cook carrots. And it seems to me that all of them point to the possibility that this something, which matters so much, is a deeper and different sort of "truth" than those more mundane matters. What's more, if it's a different sort of truth, we might expect that to grasp it we might need a different sort of knowing. We shall come to that, too, in due course.

We live, in fact, in a highly complex world, within which we humans are probably the most complex things of all. I once heard a great contemporary scientist say that whether we are looking into a microscope at the smallest objects we can discern, or gazing through a telescope at the vast recesses of outer space, the most interesting thing in the world remains that which is two inches or so on the near side of the lens—in other words, the human brain, including mind, imagination, memory, will, personality, and the thousand other things which we think of as separate faculties but which all, in their different ways, interlock as functions of our complex personal identity. We should expect the world and our relation to it to be at least as complex as we are. If there is a God, we should expect such a being to be at least as complex again.

I say this because people often grumble as soon as a discussion about the meaning of human life, or the possibility of God, moves away from quite simple ideas and becomes more complicated. Any world in which there are such things as music and sex, laughter and tears, mountains and mathematics, eagles and earthworms, statues and symphonies and snowflakes and sunsets—and in which we humans find ourselves in the middle of it all—is bound to be a world in which the quest for truth, for reality, for what we can be sure of, is infinitely more complicated than simple yes-and-no questions will allow. There is appropriate complexity along with appropriate simplicity. The more we learn, the more we discover that we humans are fantastically complicated creatures. Yet, on the other hand, human life is full of moments when we know that things are also very, very simple.

Think about it. The moment of birth; the moment of death; the joy of love; the discovery of vocation; the onset of life-threatening illness; the overwhelming pain and anger that sometimes sweep us off our feet. At such times the multiple complexities of our humanness gather themselves together and form one simple great exclamation mark, or (as it may be) one simple great question mark—a shout of joy or a cry of pain, a burst of laughter or a bursting into tears. Suddenly the rich harmony of our genetic package seems to sing in unison, and say, for good or ill, This is it.

We honor and celebrate our complexity and our simplicity by continually doing five things. We tell stories. We act out rituals. We create beauty. We work in communities. We think out beliefs. No doubt you might think of more, but that's enough for the moment. In and through all these things run the threads of love and pain, fear and faith, worship and doubt, the quest for justice, the thirst for spirituality, and the promise and problem of human relationship. And if there's any such thing as "truth," in some absolute sense, it must relate to, and make sense of, all this and more.

Stories, rituals, beauty, work, belief. I'm not talking just about
the novelist, the playwright, the artist, the industrialist, the philosopher. They are the *specialists* in the different areas. I'm talking about
all of us. And I'm not talking just about the special incidents—the
story of your life-changing moment, the ritual of a family wedding,
and so on. I'm talking about the ordinary moments. You come
home from a day's work. You tell stories about what has happened.
You listen to more stories on television or radio. You go through
the simple but profound ritual of cooking a meal, laying the table,
doing the thousand familiar things that say, This is who we are (or,
if you're alone, This is who I am). This is where we are ourselves.
You arrange a bunch of flowers or tidy a room. And from time to
time you discuss the meaning of it all.

Take away any of these elements, as frequently happens—take
away stories, rituals, beauty, work, or belief—and human life is
diminished. In a million ways, small and great, our highly complex
lives are made up of the interplay of these things. The multiple elements of life we noted a moment ago tie them all together in an
ever-changing kaleidoscopic pattern.

That's the complex world to which the Christian story is
addressed, the world of which it claims to make sense. Within that
complexity, we should be careful how we use the word "truth."

Over the last generation in Western culture, truth has been like
the rope in a tug-of-war contest. On the one hand, some want to
reduce all truth to "facts," things which can be proved in the way
you can prove that oil is lighter than water, or even that two and
two make four. On the other hand, some believe that all truth is
relative, and that all claims to truth are merely coded claims to
power. Ordinary mortals, dimly aware of this tug-of-war, and its
social, cultural, and political spin-offs, may well feel some uncer-
tainty about what truth is, while still knowing that it matters.

The sort of thing we could and should mean by "truth" will
vary according to what we're talking about. If I want to go into
town, it matters whether the person who has told me to take the

number 53 bus is speaking the truth or not. But by no means all truth is of that kind, or testable in the same way. If there's any truth lying behind the quest for justice, it is that the world isn't meant to be morally chaotic; but what do we mean by "meant," and how would we know? If there's any truth in the thirst for spirituality, it could be simply that humans find satisfaction in exploring a "spiritual" dimension to their lives, or it could be that we are made for relationship with another Being who can only be known that way. And, talking of relationships, the "truth" of a relationship is in the relationship itself, in being "true to" one another, which is considerably more than (though presumably it includes) telling each other the truth about the number 53 bus. As for beauty, we cannot collapse "truth" into "beauty" without running the risk of deconstructing truth by pointing out, as we did earlier, the fragility and ambiguity of the beauty we know here and now.

What we mean by "know" is likewise in need of further investigation. To "know" the deeper kinds of truth we have been hinting at is much more like "knowing" a person—something which takes a long time, a lot of trust, and a good deal of trial and error—and less like "knowing" about the right bus to take into town. It's a kind of knowing in which the subject and the object are intertwined, so that you could never say that it was either purely subjective or purely objective.

One good word for this deeper and richer kind of knowing, the kind that goes with the deeper and richer kind of truth, is "love." But before we can get to that we must take a deep breath and plunge into the center of the story which, according to the Christian tradition, makes sense of our longing for justice, spirituality, relationship, and beauty, and indeed truth and love. We must begin to talk about God. Which is like saying that we must learn to stare at the sun.

Part Two

Staring at the Sun

Five

God

The Christian story claims to be the true story about God and the world.

As such, it offers itself as the explanation of the voice whose echo we hear in the search for justice, the quest for spirituality, the longing for relationship, the yearning for beauty. None of these by itself points directly to God—to any God, let alone the Christian God. At best, they wave their arms in a rather general direction, like someone in a cave who hears an echoing voice but has no idea where it's coming from.

To change the picture, the reflections we have offered so far are like paths which appear to lead to the center of a maze, and which do indeed bring us near the goal—but then leave us tantalizingly short, separated from the center by a thick hedge. I do not believe that they, or any other paths, lead the unaided human mind all the way from reflective atheism to Christian faith. Still less do they "prove" either the existence of God or his particular character. It isn't simply a matter of looking at all the possible pathways and discovering that none of them will quite get us where we might have wanted to go. It's a deeper problem than that. It has to do with the meaning of the word "God" itself.

Change the picture yet again. Imagine being in a lonely house out in the country, away from streetlights. Late one wintry evening, the power goes off, leaving everything blacked out for miles around. You remember having left a box of matches on the coffee table and grope your way to them. Striking one match after another, you find your way to the pantry shelf that holds an assortment of candles. The candle you light keeps you going while you hunt around for a flashlight.

All that makes sense. Matches, candles, and flashlights are things we can use to help us see in the dark. What makes no sense, when at last it's nearly morning, is to go out with either matches, candles, or flashlight to see if the sun has risen yet.

A great many arguments about God—God's existence, God's nature, God's actions in the world—run the risk of being like pointing a flashlight toward the sky to see if the sun is shining. It is all too easy to make the mistake of speaking and thinking as though God (if there is a God) might be a being, an entity, within our world, accessible to our interested study in the same sort of way we might study music or mathematics, open to our investigation by the same sort of techniques we use for objects and entities within our world. When Yuri Gagarin, the first Soviet cosmonaut, landed after orbiting the earth a few times, he declared that he had disproved the existence of God. He had been up there, he said, and had seen no sign of him. Some Christians pointed out that Gagarin had seen plenty of signs of God, if only the cosmonaut had known how to interpret them. The difficulty is that speaking of God in anything like the Christian sense is like staring into the sun. It's dazzling. It's easier, actually, to look away from the sun itself and to enjoy the fact that, once it's well and truly risen, you can see everything else clearly.

Part of the problem lies in the word we use. The English word "God," with or without a capital G, does double duty. First, it's a common noun (like "chair," "table," "dog," and "cat"), denoting a divine being. When we say, "What kind of gods did the early Egyptians believe in?" we all understand the question: there are, we take it, various possible types of gods, and indeed goddesses, worshipped and spoken of in various traditions. But the word "God" and its equivalents is also regularly used, in those languages affected by the great monotheistic religions (Judaism, Christianity, and Islam), as a kind of proper or personal name. If you ask someone, even in today's Western world, "Do you believe in God?" the question will be heard (and presumably intended) in the sense of "the one God of the Judeo-Christian tradition." That's quite a different question from, "Do you believe in *a* god?"

Of course, many people today have only the sketchiest idea of what Christianity has said about God. Sometimes, when people are asked whether they believe in God, they picture an image that few sensible people could believe in if they tried for a week: an old man with a long white beard (as, perhaps, in some of William Blake's remarkable drawings), sitting on a cloud, looking down angrily at the mess we humans are making of the world. That imagery has only a loose relationship to any serious Christian reflection, yet it's remarkable how many people think that that is what we Christians are talking about when we say the word "God."

But the point remains: our lines of inquiry, our probing and questioning, may perhaps lead us in the direction where God might be found, but they cannot break through and claim to have grasped God all by themselves. Just as no spaceship could ever fly far enough to glimpse God, since (if such a being exists, and if he is remotely like the great monotheistic religions have supposed) he isn't an object within our universe, likewise no human argument could ever, as it were, get God in a corner, pin him down, and force him to submit to human inspection.

It is part of the Christian story that there was a moment when God was indeed pinned down, subjected not just to human inspection but to trial, torture, imprisonment, and death. But that is so strange a claim that it must wait for fuller discussion later. In any case, the activities of those who ill-treated Jesus of Nazareth are hardly meant to serve as a model for those who, having read thus far, might be inclined to ask whether the echoes of a voice to which they have been listening might, if followed carefully enough, lead them to the voice itself.

To borrow an image from another part of the Christian story, those who come with arguments to prove (or perhaps to disprove) the existence of God are always in danger of the kind of surprise received by the women who went to Jesus's tomb on Easter morning. They had gone to do what was appropriate for a dead friend, leader, and would-be Messiah. But he was up (so to speak) before them. Their actions were indeed appropriate, granted where they were starting from, but his resurrection put everything into a new light. We shall explore that light in due course, since it illuminates not only the question about Jesus but (again like the sun) everything else as well. The point at present is that, since God (if he exists) is not an object within our world, or even an idea within our *intellectual* world, we can probe toward the center of the maze as much as we like but we shall never reach that center by our own efforts.

But suppose that God, if there is a God, were to come bursting out of the center of the maze on his own initiative? That, after all, is what the great monotheistic traditions have said. To get our minds around that possibility we shall have to take a step sideways and consider more carefully what we are talking about. If God isn't up in the sky, where is he?

God in Heaven?

"God is in heaven," says one of the more hard-nosed biblical writers, "and you are upon earth; so let your words be few" (Ecclesiastes 5:2). That comes as a warning to those of us who write and speak for a living, but it highlights what the biblical tradition always insists upon: that if we are to think of God "living" anywhere, that place is known as "heaven."

Two misunderstandings need clearing up at once. First, despite what some later theologians seem to have imagined, the ancient biblical writers did not suppose that, had they been able to travel in space, they would have come sooner or later to the place where

God lived. Granted, the word "heaven" in Hebrew and Greek can mean, effectively, "the sky"; but the biblical writers move more effortlessly than most modern readers between that meaning (a location within the world of space, time, and matter) and the regular meaning of "God's dwelling place"—that is, a different *sort* of "location" altogether. (This is not to be confused with the question of "literal" and "metaphorical" meanings, which is discussed in Chapter Fourteen.) "Heaven" in this latter, very common biblical sense is God's space *as opposed to* our space, not God's location *within* our space-time universe. The question is then whether God's space and our space intersect; and if so how, when, and where.

The second misunderstanding comes about because the word "heaven" is regularly used, misleadingly but very frequently, to mean "the place where God's people will be with him, in blissful happiness, after they die." It has thus come to be thought of as a destination, a final resting place for the souls of the blessed; and, as such, it has regularly been paired with its assumed opposite, "hell." But "heaven" has this meaning, not because, in the earliest Christian traditions, it was the final destination of the redeemed, but because the word offers a way of talking about where God always is, so that the promise held out in the phrase "going to heaven" is more or less exactly "going to be with God in the place where he's been all along." Thus "heaven" is not just a future reality, but a present one. And we then meet the same question as before, from a different angle: How does this "place," this "location" (I use quote marks because I am *not* referring to a place or location within our world of space, time, and matter) interact with our world? Indeed, does it do so at all?

In the Bible, our world is called "earth." Just as "heaven" can refer to the sky, but very commonly refers to God's dimension of reality as opposed to ours, so the word "earth" can refer to the actual soil beneath our feet, but also regularly refers, as in the earlier quotation from Ecclesiastes, to our space, our dimension of reality, as opposed to God's. "The heavens are the Lord's heavens, but the earth he has given to human beings" (Psalm 115:16). Thus, though the Bible can speak of places "under the earth" in addition to heaven and earth themselves, the normal pairing is the one we find in the first line of the Bible: "In the beginning God created the heavens and the earth."

Getting this straight provides the setting in which we can address the underlying question more directly. How do heaven and earth, God's space and our space, relate to one another?

Heaven and Earth: The Puzzle

There are three basic ways (with variations) in which we can imagine God's space and ours relating to one another. Many thinkers, by no means all within the Judeo-Christian tradition, have seen things this way. Many people today know the basics of complex subjects like economics or nuclear physics; yet many, including many Christians, have little idea about the basic options in theology.

Option One is to slide the two spaces together. God's space and ours, in this option, are basically the same; or, to put it another way, they are two ways of talking about the same thing. Since God, as seen in this option, doesn't hide in a corner of his territory, but fills it all with his presence, God is everywhere, and—watch this carefully—everywhere is God. Or, if you like, God is everything, and everything is God.

This option is known as "pantheism." It was popular in the ancient Greek and Roman worlds of the first century, mainly through the philosophy called "Stoicism," and after centuries in decline it has become increasingly popular in our own times. Originally, it was a way of rolling into one all the old gods worshipped in Greece and Rome—Zeus (or Jupiter), Poseidon (or Neptune), and so on. There were gods of the sea and the sky, gods of fire, of love, of war; the trees were divine, the rivers were divine—everything was divine or at least had the spark of divinity about it. That kind of polytheism is messy and complicated. Many ancient thinkers suggested that it was easier, neater, and cleaner to suppose that "the divine" is a force which permeates everything. The main obligation on human beings is then to get in touch with, and in tune with, the divinity within themselves and within the world around. Many today find this perspective very appealing.

Proper pantheism is quite demanding. You really have to try hard to believe that there's divinity in *everything,* including wasps, mosquitoes, cancer cells, tsunamis, and hurricanes. That's at least partly why some thinkers today have opted for a subtle variation, called "pan*en*theism"—the view that, though everything may not be divine as such, everything that exists is "within" God ("pan" = "everything," "en" = "in," "theos" = "God"). There are some things to be said in favor of this, but the strong points of panentheism can better be understood from within Option Three (see below).

The problem with pantheism, and to a large extent with panentheism, is that it can't cope with evil. Within the multigodded paganism out of which pantheism grew, when something went wrong you could blame it on a god or goddess who was out to get you, perhaps because you'd forgotten to buy him or her off. But when everything (including yourself) shares in, or lives within, divinity, there's no higher court of appeal when something bad happens. Nobody can come and rescue you. The world and "the divine" are what they are, and you'd better get used to it. The only final answer (given by many Stoics in the first century, and by increasing numbers in today's Western world) is suicide.

Option Two is to hold the two spaces firmly apart. God's space and ours are a long way away from one another in this option. The gods, supposing they exist, are in their heaven, wherever and whatever that is. They're enjoying themselves—not least because they aren't involved with us here on earth. This view, too, was popular in the ancient world. It was taught, particularly, by the great poet/ philosopher Lucretius, who lived in the century before Jesus, and who expounded and developed the teaching of Epicurus from two centuries before that. For Lucretius and Epicurus, the result of this view is that human beings should get used to being alone in the world. The gods will not intervene, either to help or to harm. The right thing to do is to enjoy life as best one can. This meant being quiet, careful, and moderate. (Some have subsequently taken "Epicurean" to mean a life of sensuality and hedonism. Epicurus and his followers reckoned that sort of life didn't work. You got more genuine pleasure, they thought, from being steady and sober.)

Watch what happens once you separate the two spheres, God's and ours, in such a radical fashion. If (like many of the ancient philosophers) you were reasonably well off and could afford a nice home, good food and wine, and slaves to look after you, you could shrug your shoulders at the distant gods and still expect to do all right. But if, like the great majority of the population, your life was harsh, cruel, and often downright miserable, it was easy to believe that the world where you lived was dark, nasty, and wicked in its very essence, and that your best hope was to escape it, either by death itself (there we go again) or by some kind of super-spirituality which would enable you to enjoy a secret happy life here and now and hope for an even better one after death. That's the breeding ground for the philosophy known broadly as "Gnosticism," about which I shall have more to say later on.

Separating God's sphere and ours in the Epicurean fashion, with a distant God whom you might respect but who wasn't going to appear or *do* anything within our sphere, became very popular in the Western world of the eighteenth century (through the movement known as "Deism"), and has continued to be so in many places to this day. In fact, many people in the Western world assume that when they talk about "God" and "heaven" they're talking about a being and a place which—if they exist at all—are a long way away and have little or nothing directly to do with us. That's why, when many people say they believe in God, they will often add in the same breath that they don't go to church, they don't pray, and in fact they don't think much about God from one year's end to the next. I don't blame them. If I believed in a distant, remote God like that, I wouldn't get out of bed on a Sunday morning either.

The real problem with Epicureanism in the ancient world, and Deism in ours, is that it has to plug its ears to all those echoing voices we were talking about earlier in this book. Actually, that's not so difficult in today's busy and noisy world. It's quite easy, in fact, when you're sitting in front of the television or hooked up to a portable stereo, one hand glued to the cell phone for text messaging, the other clutching a mug of specialist coffee . . . it's quite easy to be a modern Epicurean. But turn the machines off, read a different kind of book, wander out under the night sky, and see what happens. You might start wondering about Option Three.

Heaven and Earth: Overlapping, Interlocking

Option Three is what we find within classic Judaism and Christianity. Heaven and earth are not coterminous, in this option. Nor are they separated by a great gulf. Instead, they overlap and interlock in a number of different ways. This can seem initially confusing, after the clean either/or of pantheism and Deism; but it is the kind of confusion we should welcome. It embraces the complexity which we ought to expect if human life is in fact as intricate and many-sided as we have seen in the earlier chapters. It is easy to think you have mastered Shakespeare's plays if all you have on the shelf is the comedies. When someone brings you all the other plays as well—the tragedies and the history plays, plus a volume or two of the great man's poetry for good measure—you will complain that things are now getting confused and highly complex. But you are actually closer to understanding Shakespeare, not further away.

Something like that happens when we turn from the ancient and modern philosophies of the non-Jewish world to the world of the Old Testament, the world of the ancient Israelites, the world that still forms the foundation for those two estranged sisters, Judaism and Christianity, and to a lesser extent Islam. The Old Testament insists that God belongs in heaven and we on earth. Yet it shows over and over again that the two spheres do indeed overlap, so that God makes his presence known, seen, and heard within the sphere of earth.

This strange presence is the subplot of many of the early stories. Abraham keeps meeting God. Jacob sees a ladder between heaven and earth, with angels going to and fro. Moses discovers that he's standing on holy ground—a place, in other words, where (for the moment at least) heaven and earth intersect—as he watches the burning bush. Then, when Moses leads the Israelites out of Egypt, God goes before them in a pillar of cloud by day and a pillar of fire by night. When they come to Mount Sinai, God appears on the summit, giving Moses the Law. And God continues—under protest, because of Israel's radical misbehavior—to accompany them on their journey to the Promised Land. Indeed, a considerable part of the biblical book of Exodus is devoted (rather to our surprise, after the fast-paced narrative of the first half of the book) to a description of the portable shrine where God will condescend to dwell in the midst of his people. Evocatively, it is called "the Tent of Meeting." It is a place where heaven and earth come together.

The main focus of ancient Israelite belief in the overlap of heaven and earth was the Temple in Jerusalem. To begin with, when they first lived in the land, the sign of God's presence was the "Ark of the Covenant," a wooden box containing the stone tablets of the Law and sundry other sacred objects. That box was still kept in a holy tent. But when David made Jerusalem his capital, the civic and political center of the whole nation, he planned a new project, which his son Solomon then constructed: a great Temple, the single sanctuary for the whole nation, the place where Israel's God would now make his home forever.

From that moment on, the Temple on Mount Zion in Jerusalem was the primary place, according to Israelite tradition, where heaven and earth met. "The Lord has chosen Zion; he has desired it for his residence: 'This is my resting-place forever; here will I live, for I have desired it'" (Psalm 132:13–14).When Israel's God blessed people, he did so *from* Zion.When they were far away, they would turn and pray *toward* the Temple.When pilgrims and worshippers went up to Jerusalem and into the Temple to worship and offer sacrifices, they wouldn't have said that it was *as though* they were going into heaven.They would have said that they were going to the place where heaven and earth overlapped and interlocked.

This sense of overlap between heaven and earth, and the sense of God thereby being present on earth without having to leave heaven, lies at the heart of Jewish and early Christian theology. Many confusions arise at exactly this point. If you try to think of the main Christian affirmations within any other scheme of thought (within, say, Options One or Two), they seem strange, awkward, perhaps even self-contradictory. Put them back in their proper context, though, and they make remarkable sense.

The belief in heaven and earth as quasi-independent but mysteriously overlapping spheres goes a long way toward explaining several otherwise puzzling things in ancient Israelite and early Christian thought and life. Take creation itself, coupled with the notion of God's action in the world.

For the pantheist, God and the world are basically the same thing: the world is, if you like, God's self-expression. For the Deist, the world may indeed have been made by God (or the gods), but there is now no contact between divine and human. The Deist God wouldn't dream of "intervening" within the created order; to do so would be untidy, a kind of category mistake. But for the ancient Israelite and the early Christian, the creation of the world was the free outpouring of God's powerful love. The one true God made a world that was other than himself, because that is what love delights to do. And, having made such a world, he has remained in a close, dynamic, and intimate relationship with it, without in any way being contained within it or having it contained within himself. To speak of God's action in the world, of heaven's action (if you like) on earth—and Christians speak of this every time they say the

Lord's Prayer—is to speak not of an awkward metaphysical blun-
der, nor of a "miracle" in the sense of a random invasion of earth
by alien ("supernatural"?) forces, but to speak of the loving Creator
acting within the creation which has never lacked the signs of his
presence. It is to speak, in fact, of such actions as might be expected to leave echoes. Echoes of a voice.

In particular, this God appears to take very seriously the fact that
his beloved creation has become corrupt, has rebelled and is suffering the consequences. This is something the pantheist can't cope
with (as we saw). Even panentheism has a hard time giving a serious account of the radical nature of evil, let alone of what a good
God might do about it. And for the Deist God, there is simply a
shrug of the shoulders. If the world is in a mess, why should God
care? Hadn't we better try to sort things out by ourselves? Many
popular misconceptions of Christian faith make the mistake at this
point of trying to fit Christian belief into a residual Deist framework. They depict a distant and austere God suddenly deciding to
do something after all, and so sending his own Son to teach us how
to escape our sphere and go and live in God's instead, and then
condemning his Son to a cruel fate to satisfy some obscure and
rather arbitrary requirement.

To understand why that is such a travesty, and to get our minds
around the framework within which the Christian story makes the
sense it does, we must examine more closely the rescue operation
which, in both Jewish and Christian tradition, the true God has
mounted. What happens when the God of Option Three decides
to deal with evil?

The answer, to the surprise of many in today's world, has to
do with God's calling of Abraham. But before we get there we
had better say one more word about the ancient Jewish belief
about God.

The Name of God

At some point along the way—it's hard to be sure historically when exactly this happened—the ancient Israelites came to know their God by a special name.

This name was regarded as so special, so holy, that by the time of Jesus, and perhaps for some centuries before that, they were not allowed to say it out loud. (One exception was made: the high priest, once a year, would pronounce God's special name in a place called the Holy of Holies at the heart of the Temple.) Since Hebrew script only used consonants, we can't even be sure how the name was meant to be pronounced: the consonants are YHWH, and the best guess we have at how they were pronounced is "Yahweh." Orthodox Jews to this day won't speak this name; they often refer to God simply as "the Name," *HaShem*. Neither will they write it. Sometimes they write even the generic word "God" as "G–d," to make the same point.

Like most ancient names, YHWH had a meaning. It seems to have meant "I am who I am," or "I will be who I will be." This God, the name suggests, can't be defined in terms of anything or anyone else. It isn't the case that there is such a thing as "divinity" and that he's simply another example, even the supreme one, of this category. Nor is it the case that all things that exist, including God, share in something we might call "being" or "existence," so that God would then be the supremely existing being. Rather, he is who he is. He is his own category, not part of a larger one. That is why we can't expect to mount a ladder of arguments from our world and end up in his, any more than we might expect to mount a ladder of moral achievement and end up making ourselves good enough to stand in his presence.

With God's name there is another confusion which we must sort out. Because God's personal name was not to be spoken, the ancient Israelites developed a technique for avoiding doing so when reading their scriptures. When they came to the word YHWH, they would say ADONAI (which means "my Lord") instead. As a way of reminding themselves that this was what they had to do, they would sometimes write the consonants of YHWH with the vowels of ADONAI. This confused some later readers, who tried to say the two words together. With a bit of a stretch (and because some letters were interchangeable, including Y with J and W with V), they created the hybrid JEHOVAH. No ancient Israelite or early Christian would have recognized this word.

Almost all English translations of the Old Testament have continued the practice of discouraging people from pronouncing God's personal name. Instead, when the word occurs, it is normally translated "the Lord." Sometimes this is written in small capitals, as in "the LORD." This is doubly confusing, and anyone who wants to understand what Judaism, let alone Christianity, believes about God had better get their mind around the problem.

From very early times (indeed, according to the gospels, since Jesus's own lifetime) Christians have referred to Jesus himself as "the Lord." In early Christian speech this phrase carried at least three meanings: (a) "the master," "the one whose servants we are," "the one we've promised to obey"; (b) "the true Lord" (as opposed to Caesar, who claimed the same title); and (c) "the LORD"—that is, YHWH—as spoken of in the Old Testament. All these meanings are visible in Paul, the earliest Christian writer we have. The early Christians rejoiced in this flexibility, but for us it has become a source of confusion.

Within contemporary Western culture, under the influence of Deism, the phrase "the Lord" has shifted from referring either to Jesus specifically or to the YHWH of the Old Testament. It has become, instead, a way of referring simply to a rather distant, generalized deity, who might conceivably have something to do with Jesus but equally well might not, and would probably not have much to do with YHWH either. Thus it has come about that ancient Israelite scruples, medieval mistranslation, and fuzzy eighteenth-century thinking have combined to make it hard for us today to recapture the vital sense of what a first-century Jew would understand when thinking of YHWH, what an early Christian would be saying when speaking of Jesus or "the Lord," and how we might now properly reappropriate this whole tradition.

Still, the effort has to be made. All language about God is ultimately mysterious, but that is no excuse for sloppy or woolly thinking. And since the title "Lord" was one of the favorite early Christian ways of speaking about Jesus, it is vital that we get clear on the point.

To take this any further we need to look more closely at the people who believed themselves called by the one true God, YHWH, to be his special people for the sake of the world—the people who spoke of his rescue operation for the whole cosmos and thought of themselves as the agents of that plan. It is within the story of this people that we can make sense of the story of Jesus of Nazareth himself, the center and focal point of Christian faith. And it is when we understand Jesus, I shall suggest, that we begin to recognize the voice whose echoes we have heard in the longing for justice, the hunger for spirituality and relationship, and the delight in beauty.

Six

Israel

Why should we spend an entire chapter discussing the nation within which, as a matter of historical accident, Jesus of Nazareth just happened to be born?

No early Christian would have thought of it like that. It is a measure of how far the Christian world has traveled away from its roots that such a question could even be asked. It is fundamental to the Christian worldview in its truest form that what happened in Jesus of Nazareth was the very climax of the long story of Israel. Trying to understand Jesus without understanding what that story was, how it worked, and what it meant is like trying to understand why someone is hitting a ball with a stick without knowing what baseball, or indeed cricket, is all about.

There are, of course, formidable difficulties for a Christian in saying anything very much about Israel—whether ancient Israel, the Israel of Jesus's day, or modern Israel. A few weeks ago I visited Yad Vashem (which means "a memorial and a name"), the Holocaust memorial in Jerusalem. I read, not for the first time, the scribbled testimony of a Jewish man who, with dozens of others, had been stuffed into an airless cattle truck and shipped off, already in a living hell, to his death. I wandered around the quarry where, carved in solid rock, are the names of European towns from which thousands of Jews were rounded up and carted off to be butchered. Everything any of us might say about the Jewish people is tinged with sorrow, a shaking of the head, and a deep shame that from within European culture (which some still think of as "Christian"!) such a thing could even have been thinkable, let alone doable.

But this doesn't mean that there is nothing to say. Indeed, to say nothing about the Jewish story, within which Jesus made the sense he did, is to connive at that anti-Judaism which had been latent for many years before Hitler turned it into reality. We must speak, even though we tremble as we do so.

Nor is it only contemporary sensibilities that get in the way. There are huge historical debates over how much we can really know about Abraham, Moses, David, and the rest. Was there *really* an "exodus" from Egypt? The biblical writers appear to be telling us about events in the Late Bronze Age and Early Iron Age (together, roughly 1500–1000 BC). Were the accounts written at the time and edited later, or were they written five or six hundred years later; and, if the latter, were they based on solid traditional material or made up out of thin air?

At the risk of begging several questions, I am going to tell the story *the way Jews of Jesus's day might have told it,* or at least in one such way. Here we are on safe ground. We have the Old Testament itself, in Hebrew (with a few parts in Aramaic). We have its Greek translation, commonly called the Septuagint, written in the two or three centuries before the time of Jesus. We also have several books from within a century or two of Jesus's day, which retell some or all of the biblical story and which highlight certain features for particular emphasis. The best known of these is the massive *Antiquities of the Jews* by the brilliant (if maverick) Flavius Josephus, a Jewish aristocrat who fought in the war against Rome in the mid-60s, changed sides, worked for the Romans, and retired to Rome on a state pension after the destruction of Jerusalem in the year AD 70. Telling the story the way a first-century Jew might have seen it not only avoids the massive historical questions that still rage around the early period, but prepares us for understanding why Jesus of Nazareth said and did what he did, and why this had the impact it had.

We have already spoken about the very beginning of the story. We jump now to one of the key early moments: the call of Abraham. Or rather, the tragicomic incident which precedes it and prepares us for it.

The Call of Abraham

"Oh, so you've built a *tower*, have you? Whatever will you think of next?" That's the tone of voice we find in Genesis 11, when God comments, sardonically, on the pathetic little efforts of human beings to make themselves big and important. The story has gone from bad to worse: from rebellion in the Garden of Eden (chapter 3) to the first murder (chapter 4) to widespread violence (chapter 6), and now to the crazy idea of building a tower—what we now call the Tower of Babel—with its top reaching right up to heaven (chapter 11). Those who were supposed to be reflecting God's image into the world—that is, human beings—are instead looking into mirrors of their own; and they both like and are frightened by what they see. Arrogant and insecure, they have become self-important. God scatters them across the face of the earth, confusing their languages so that they can no longer pursue their grandiose projects.

The story of the Tower of Babel is an account of a world given to injustice, spurious types of spirituality (trying to stretch up to heaven by our own efforts), failed relationships, and the creation of buildings whose urban ugliness speaks of human pride rather than the nurturing of beauty. It all sounds worryingly familiar. That is the scene within which, in Genesis 12, we find the great turning point. God calls Abram (his name is lengthened to Abraham five chapters later) and makes spectacular promises to him:

> I will make of you a great nation, and I will bless you, and make your name great, so that you will be a blessing. I will bless those who bless you, and the one who curses you I will

curse; and in you all the families of the earth shall be blessed.
(12:2–3)

The last line is the vital one. The families of the earth have
become divided and confused, and are ruining their own lives and
that of the world at large. Abraham and his descendants are somehow to be the means of God putting things to rights, the spearhead
of God's rescue operation.

Somehow. At first it seems like a crazy, impossible idea. But the
promise is repeated and developed over the subsequent chapters. In
particular, God makes a "covenant" with Abraham: a deal, a binding
agreement, a promise into which both God and Abraham are locked
forever afterward. It isn't exactly a "contract"; that would imply some
kind of equality between the parties, but God remains firmly in
control of this agreement from start to finish. Sometimes God is
described as the father, and Israel as the firstborn son; sometimes
God is the master, Israel the servant. Sometimes, hauntingly, the covenant is spoken of in terms of a marriage, with God as bridegroom
and Israel as bride. We need all these images (remembering, of course,
that they are only images, and that they are taken from a world quite
different from our own) to get the full flavor of the story.

The point is that God's covenant with Abraham is seen as a rock-
solid commitment on the part of the world's Creator that he will
be the God of Abraham and his family. *Through* Abraham and his
family, God will bless the whole world. Shimmering like a mirage
in the deserts through which Abraham wandered was the vision of
a new world, a rescued world, a world blessed by the Creator once
more, a world of justice, where God and his people would live in
harmony, where human relationships would flourish, where beauty would triumph over ugliness. It would be a world in which the
voices that echo in all human consciousness would blend together
and be heard as the voice of the living God.

The covenant may have been rock-solid on God's part, but as
Genesis tells the story, it was anything but solid on Abraham's part.

Right from the beginning we run into the problem that will haunt the narrative throughout: What happens when the lifeboat which sets off to rescue the wrecked ship is itself trapped between the rocks and the waves, itself in need of rescue? What happens when the people through whom God wants to mount his rescue operation, the people through whom he intends to set the world to rights, themselves need rescuing, themselves need putting to rights? What happens when Israel becomes part of the problem, not just the bearer of the solution? As cheerful old Rabbi Lionel Blue once said on the radio, "Jews are just like everyone else, only more so." The Old Testament underlines that on page after page.

But if the God who made the world out of free, boundless, energetic love now sees his world in rebellion, and his rescue operation flawed because of the people he has chosen to carry it out, what is he to do? He can't now say that it was all a mistake. (The closest God comes to that is with the Flood in Genesis 6–8; but part of the point there is that God rescues Noah and the nonhuman creation, in order that things may start up again.) Instead, he acts from within the creation itself, with all the ambiguities and paradoxes which that involves, in order to deal with the multiple problems that have resulted from human rebellion, and so to restore creation itself. And he acts from within the covenant people themselves, to complete the rescue operation and fulfill its original purpose.

All this explains why the story of Israel carries at its heart a single theme, repeated like a Wagnerian leitmotif over and over in different contexts and from different points of view. It is the story of going away and coming back home again: of slavery and exodus, of exile and restoration. It is the story which Jesus of Nazareth consciously told in his words, in his actions, and supremely in his death and resurrection.

Exile and Homecoming

It was perhaps inevitable that the Jewish storytellers who produced the Old Testament should see going-away-and-coming-back-again as their main motif. The main parts of the Hebrew scriptures most likely reached their final form when the Jews were in exile in Babylon, living with the sorrow of being away not only from their homeland but from the Temple where YHWH had promised to be with them ("How can we sing YHWH's songs," complains one of the poets of that time, "in a strange land?" [Psalm 137:4]). The irony of Abraham's family living in Babylon, the land of the Tower of Babel, was not lost on them. But they knew what to hope for. They had been in exile before. That was the central theme of all their stories.

It began, in fact, with Abraham himself, who as part of his nomadic life goes down to Egypt for a while—and nearly gets stuck there. Frightened for his life, he tells a lie, saying that Sarah, his wife, is his sister. (It's a white lie, because she was in fact his half sister.) He is then allowed to go. That story is told immediately after the first great promise has been made to Abraham, as though to say, "See? No sooner has God given him this great future than he almost throws it away."

The pattern repeats itself in all sorts of ways. Jacob, for example, cheats his brother Esau and has to flee eastward, but he eventually returns home to face his brother and, more important, to wrestle with God (Genesis 32). There is a great deal of justice, spirituality, and restored relationship echoing around that story, echoes of larger themes that writers and editors never forgot.

But all the lines in Genesis lead to the going-away-and-coming-back-again story of Joseph. He is taken to Egypt and sold as a slave, but he soon earns favor and becomes a successful man. His entire family eventually joins him in Egypt because of famine back home, and he's able to help them. Within a generation—but after Joseph's death—the favored status given to the family changes, and they, too, are reduced to slavery. Then, at the moment when things reach their worst, God hears their cry for help and promises to lead his people out of slavery, to give them freedom in their own land. That is one of the great moments in Jewish and Christian memory, drawing together God's faithfulness to the promises to Abraham, God's compassion for his people when they are suffering, God's promise of rescue, freedom, and hope, and above all the unveiling of God's name and its significance:

> God said to Moses, "I AM WHO I AM." He said further, "Thus you shall say to the Israelites, 'I AM has sent me to you.'" God also said to Moses, "Thus you shall say to the Israelites, 'YHWH, the God of your ancestors, the God of Abraham, the God of Isaac, and the God of Jacob, has sent me to you. This is my name forever, and this is my title for all generations. . . . I declare that I will bring you up out of the misery of Egypt, to the land . . . flowing with milk and honey.'" (Exodus 3:14–17)

And it happened. God judged the pagan Egyptians and rescued his people. That is the story of Passover, one of the great Jewish festivals to this day.

It wasn't (to put it mildly) as straightforward as it might have been. But eventually the Israelites reached the land they had been promised. There, too, things went both well and badly, as other local tribes ruled over them and other liberators rose up to set them free. It was out of that experience of semi-chaos that the people asked for a king; and, after a false start with Saul, David emerged, hailed as "the man after God's own heart." Like Abraham, he, too, followed his own heart, but with disastrous results. The centerpiece of what should have been the story of his kingdom being established was instead the story of his running away from his rebel son, Absalom. Again the pattern repeats itself: David goes into exile, and returns sadder and wiser. But within two generations his kingdom has been divided. Two centuries after that, the larger segment, the northern kingdom that took the name "Israel" (over against the southern kingdom, "Judah"), had been devastated by Assyria and forcibly evacuated. This time the storyline ran out of steam. There was no return home.

The kingdom of Judah struggled on, focused on Jerusalem. But as Assyria became weaker, a darker enemy arose: Babylon, which established its huge, sprawling, all-conquering empire, and swallowed up the little state of Judah like a sea monster gulping down a minnow. Jerusalem was destroyed, Temple and all; the family of David was disgraced and decimated. The people who had sung the songs of YHWH found that the words stuck in their throats in a strange, hostile land.

And then it happened again: a homecoming. After seventy years had passed, Babylon fell to Persia, and the new Persian ruler decided to send the Jews home. Jerusalem was reinhabited, and the Temple was rebuilt. "When YHWH restored the fortunes of Zion," wrote a poet, hardly able to speak for sheer astonished delight, "we were like people who dream; our mouth was filled with laughter, and our tongue with shouts of joy" (Psalm 126:1–2). Exile and homecoming, the great theme of Jewish storytelling from that day to this, was cemented into the consciousness of the people who once again began to go up to Jerusalem in the belief that heaven and earth overlapped in the Temple, that there YHWH would meet with his people in forgiveness and fellowship, that his project to rescue his people and set the world to rights was still on course despite everything.

Rescued from the Monsters

But it wasn't the same. At least, not the same as it had been in the world of David and Solomon, when Israel was free and independent, when the surrounding nations were subservient, when people came from far away to see the beauty of Jerusalem and to hear the wisdom of the king. Israel had come back from Babylon; but, as some writers of the time put it, they were still slaves—in their own land! Empire followed empire: Persia, Egypt, Greece, Syria, finally Rome. Was this, wondered the Jewish people, what homecoming was really all about? Was this what it would look like when God rescued his people and put the world to rights?

Somewhere in the middle of this period a learned Jew compiled a book of stories about Jewish heroes and visionaries under foreign rule. The book, named Daniel after its principal character, emphasizes the undying hope that the whole world will somehow be brought to order under the kingship of the one creator God, YHWH, the God of Abraham. The book makes it clear, though, that this promise had taken longer to fulfill than most Jews had imagined. Yes, they had indeed come home from Babylon; but in a deeper sense their "exile" would last not for a mere seventy years but for "seventy weeks of years"—in other words, seventy times seven, or 490 (Daniel 9:24). We are familiar with people in our own day who use old prophecies to calculate current events. Lots of Jews in what we call the last two centuries BC tried to work out, on the basis of this prophecy, when their exile would be over, when God would rescue them and set the world to rights.

This is where we meet a belief which goes on to become one of the leading themes of early Christianity. Earlier Israelite poets and prophets had declared that their God would become truly king of the world. Daniel carves this belief into the storyline of Israel's exile and restoration, going away and coming back home. When God's people are finally rescued—when, in other words, the oppressing pagans are overthrown and Israel is free at last—that will be the time when the true God will fulfill all his promises, judge the whole world, and make all things right. The "monsters" who have attacked God's people will be condemned, and the one who will judge them will be a strange, human figure, "one like a son of man"—one who represents God's people, vindicated after suffering (Daniel 7). That will be the coming of "God's kingdom," God's sovereign rule over the world, judging evil and putting everything straight. And with that, we are almost ready to look at the man who made that the theme of his life's work.

The Hope of Israel

Almost, but not quite. There are four themes that swirl around the story of Israel as we find it both in the scriptural writings and in later Jewish books—four themes that give shape and body to the story as we have outlined it.

First, the king. The spectacular promises God made to David— promises that his royal house would continue forever (2 Samuel 7)—came on the back of warnings issued by the prophet Samuel about the oppressive way all earthly kings behave (1 Samuel 8). David's own behavior, and that of his son Solomon, demonstrated Samuel's point only too well. And most of David's successors were weak or positively bad; even those who succeeded in restoring the life and worship of Israel (Hezekiah, Josiah) couldn't prevent the final catastrophe of exile. Psalm 89, one of the most majestic and haunting of the whole collection of the Psalms, states the problem as starkly as it can be put. On the one hand, God made all these great promises to David; on the other hand, it looks as though they have all come to nothing. The poem lays both halves before God, as though to say, "Well? What are you going to do about it?"

But it is out of this sense of puzzled ambiguity that there grows, in fits and starts but eventually becoming clear and emphatic, the hope that one day there might be a true king, a new sort of king, a king who would set everything right. When he takes his throne, the poor will get justice at last; creation itself will sing for joy.

> Give the king your justice, O God,
> and your righteousness to the king's son.
> May he judge your people with righteousness,
> and your poor with justice.

May the mountains yield prosperity for the people,
and the hills, in righteousness.
May he defend the cause of the poor of the people,
give deliverance to the needy, and crush the oppressor.
(Psalm 72:1–4)

This is how God's ancient promises are to be fulfilled. There will come a new king, anointed with oil and with God's own Spirit (the Hebrew for "anointed one" is "Messiah"; the Greek is "Christ"), and he will put the world back into proper order. The echoing voice that calls for justice will be answered at last.

Second, the Temple. In theory, as we have seen, the Jews believed that the Temple was the place where heaven and earth met. But by all accounts the so-called Second Temple (the Temple rebuilt after the Israelites' return from Babylon, which stood until the awful devastation of AD 70) couldn't hold a candle to its magnificent predecessor. Even the priests who worked there treated it disdainfully, as the prophet Malachi complained. Ever since David, it was the king who was supposed to build or restore the Temple, but the job wasn't being done. In the centuries immediately before Jesus, two men used Temple restoration as a means to advance their own royal claims, despite the fact that neither of them was descended from David himself.

Judas Maccabaeus enjoyed spectacular success in his rebellion against Syria in 164 BC. He overthrew the foreign tyrant and restored the Temple (which had been used for pagan worship) to its proper use. That was enough to establish his family as a royal house for a century and more. Then Herod the Great, to whom the Romans gave the title "king of the Jews" (principally because he was the most powerful warlord in the vicinity), started a massive program of rebuilding and beautifying the Temple—a program that his sons carried on after him. That work, though, wasn't enough to sustain their power. Their dynasty came to an end a few years before the Temple itself was destroyed in the year 70. But the principle was established. Part of the central task of the king, should a *true* king ever emerge, would not only be to establish justice in the world; it would also involve the proper reestablishment of the place where heaven and earth met. The deep human longing for spirituality, for access to God, would be answered at last.

Third, the Torah, the Law of Moses. It was probably during the exile in Babylon that the so-called Five Books of Moses, also known as the Torah, were edited into their final form, highlighting the ancient story of slavery and freedom, of exile and homecoming, of oppression and Passover—but also setting out the pattern of life for the people who had thus been rescued. When God frees you from slavery, said the Torah, this is how you must behave, not to earn his favor (as though you could put God in your moral debt), but to express your gratitude, your loyalty, and your determination to live by the covenant because of which God rescued you in the first place. That is the logic underlying the increasingly focused study and practice of the Torah from the Babylonian exile to the time of Jesus and beyond.

The Torah was never intended as a charter for individuals, as though anyone, anywhere, might decide to try to keep its precepts and see what would happen. It was given to a people, edited by and for that people, and applied (in the postexilic period at least) to that people; and at its heart it was about how that people would live together, under God and in harmony—that is, justice—with one another. Anthropologists have increasingly recognized that many of the taboos and customs enshrined in the Torah were, at the symbolic level at least, ways of keeping the nation together, of protecting its identity as the covenant people of the one God, especially during times of pagan threat. That is why, for instance, Judas Maccabaeus and his family revolted against Syria: the Syrians, as a specific and deliberate move, had not only desecrated the Temple with pagan worship but were doing their best to force loyal Jews to break the Torah. Both moves had the same purpose: they were ways of destroying national identity, of breaking the spirit. The Maccabean revolt was as much about the Torah as it was about the Temple. And the Torah was all about living as the people—the family—of God.

It was an answer to that cry for true relationship, with God and with one another, which echoes around every human heart.

Fourth, new creation. Daniel was not the only book to reach right back to the global promises God had made to Abraham. The great central section of the book of Isaiah speaks of God's intention, not only to restore the tribes of Jacob, but to bring light to the pagan nations as well (49:6). And it is that same book where we find, in spectacular form, the rushing together of hopes for king, Temple, and Torah, for worldwide peace, for the replanting of the Garden of Eden—for nothing short of new creation. The beauty of this new world is matched by the beauty of the ancient poetry which evokes it. Consider this sequence, taken from various parts of the book of Isaiah:

> In days to come, the mountain of YHWH's house shall be established as the highest of the mountains, and shall be raised above the hills; all the nations shall stream to it.
>
> Many peoples shall come and say, "Come, let us go up to the mountain of YHWH, to the house of the God of Jacob, that he may teach us his ways and that we may walk in his paths."
>
> For out of Zion shall go forth instruction, and the word of YHWH from Jerusalem.
>
> He shall judge between the nations, and shall arbitrate for many people; they shall beat their swords into ploughshares, and their spears into pruning hooks;
>
> Nation shall not lift up sword against nation, neither shall they learn war any more.
>
> (Isaiah 2:2–4)

The prophet is holding out a vision of peace and hope, not only for Israel but for all the nations. When YHWH finally acts to deliver his people, to reestablish Jerusalem ("Zion") as the place where he will live and reign, it won't be Israel alone that will benefit. As he promised to Abraham, back at the beginning, *through* this people the creator God will bring restoration and healing to the whole world.

More specifically, God will do this through the arrival of the ultimate king of Israel, the descendant of David (himself often referred to as "son of Jesse"). This king will possess the wisdom he will need to bring God's justice to the whole world:

A shoot shall come out from the stock of Jesse, and a branch shall grow out of his roots.

The spirit of YHWH shall rest on him, the spirit of wisdom and understanding, the spirit of counsel and might, the spirit of knowledge and the fear of YHWH.

His delight shall be in the fear of YHWH.

He shall not judge by what his eyes see, or decide by what his ears hear; but with righteousness he shall judge the poor, and decide with equity for the meek of the earth.

He shall strike the earth with the rod of his mouth, and with the breath of his lips he shall kill the wicked.

Righteousness shall be the belt around his waist, and faithfulness the belt around his loins.

The wolf shall live with the lamb, the leopard shall lie down with the kid, the calf and the lion and the fatling together, and a little child shall lead them.

The cow and the bear shall graze, their young shall lie down together; and the lion shall eat straw like the ox.

The nursing child shall play over the hole of the asp, and the weaned child shall put its hand on the adder's den.

They will not hurt or destroy on all my holy mountain; for the earth will be full of the knowledge of YHWH, as the waters cover the sea.

(Isaiah 11:1–9)

The rule of the Messiah, then, will bring peace, justice, and a completely new harmony to the whole creation. This means that an open invitation is now issued to all and sundry—anyone at all who is thirsty for justice, for spirituality, for relationships, for beauty—to come and find it here:

> Ho, everyone who thirsts, come to the waters, and you that have no money, come, buy and eat! Come, buy wine and milk without money and without price. . . .
>
> Incline your ear, and come to me; listen, so that you may live. I will make with you an everlasting covenant, my steadfast, sure love for David.
>
> See, I made him a witness to the peoples, a leader and commander for the peoples. See, you shall call nations that you do not know, and nations that do not know you shall run to you, because of YHWH your God, the Holy One of Israel, for he has glorified you. . . .
>
> For you shall go out in joy, and be led back in peace; the mountains and the hills before you shall burst into song, and all the trees of the field shall clap their hands.
>
> Instead of the thorn shall come up the cypress; instead of the brier shall come up the myrtle; and it shall be to YHWH for a memorial, for an everlasting sign that shall not be cut off.
>
> (Isaiah 55:1, 3–5, 12–13)

And the key theme, which points on from the great poetry of the Old Testament to the astonished delight of the New, is the renewal of the entire cosmos, of heaven and earth together, and the promise that in this new world all shall be well, and all manner of thing shall be well:

> For I am about to create new heavens and a new earth; the former things shall not be remembered or come to mind.
>
> But be glad and rejoice forever in what I am creating; for I am about to create Jerusalem as a joy, and its people as a delight. . . .

The wolf and the lamb shall feed together, the lion shall eat
straw like the ox; but the serpent—its food shall be dust!
They shall not hurt or destroy on all my holy mountain,
says YHWH.

(Isaiah 65:17–18, 25)

That selection of passages could have been multiplied several times over. The theme of a new Eden (the thorns and briers of
Genesis 3 replaced with beautiful shrubs) picks up one of the main
subtexts of the whole biblical story. Ultimately, the real exile, the
real leaving-home moment, was the expulsion of humankind from
the Garden of Eden. Israel's multiple exiles and restorations are
ways of reenacting that primal expulsion and symbolically express-
ing the hope for homecoming, for humankind to be restored, for
God's people to be rescued, for creation itself to be renewed. And
one of the main themes that comes back again and again, bubbling up unstoppably and echoing around the ancient prophecy as
it echoes around the human heart, is the beauty of the new creation, of Jerusalem and its inhabitants, of the landscape filled with
peaceful animals, of the mountains and hills singing for joy. Isaiah
never forgot that the reason God called Abraham in the first place
was in order to put the entire creation back to rights, to fill heaven
and earth with his glory.

Servant of YHWH

But new creation will come about only through one final and
shocking exile and restoration. The themes of king and Temple, of
Torah and new creation, of justice, spirituality, relationship, and beauty, come rushing together in the dark theme which lies at the heart
of the same book of Isaiah. The king turns into a servant, YHWH's
Servant; and the Servant must act out the fate of Israel, must *be* Israel
on behalf of the Israel that can no longer be obedient to its vocation.

The lifeboat goes out to the rescue, and the captain gets drowned in the process. That theme, developed out of the royal picture in Isaiah 11 but with the strange new twist of a vocation to obedient suffering, is laid out, step by step, in Isaiah 42, 49, 50, and 52–53. This, it appears, is how God's rescue operation must take place.

These passages do not, so to speak, "come away clean" from their context. They are woven closely together with the larger themes of the same part of the book: of YHWH's sovereignty over the nations, and his consequent overthrow of the pagan gods and those who trust in them; of his faithfulness to the covenant with Israel, despite Israel's faithlessness; of the "word" which goes out of his mouth, like his word in creation, to restore Israel, to renew the covenant, to remake the world (40:8; 55:10–11). Ultimately, it's because of the work of the Servant that the message that God is king—the message, that is, that Babylon is overthrown, that peace has come at last, that Israel is rescued and the ends of the earth shall recognize God's salvation—can be brought to Jerusalem (52:7–12). The Servant will be cast away, like Israel in exile, overwhelmed with shame, suffering, and death; and then brought through, and out the other side. This message is taken up in different, though converging, ways in other prophecies, not least in Jeremiah through the theme of the new covenant, and Ezekiel as he declares that God will cleanse his people, give them a new heart, and take them back to their own land in a rescue operation for which the only appropriate metaphor is the resurrection of the dead.

Thus Israel, gazing at the Servant, will say in wonderment, "He was wounded for our transgressions, crushed for our iniquities; upon him was the punishment that made us whole, and by his bruises we are healed" (Isaiah 53:5). At the heart of the political message that Israel's God is king, and that Babylon's gods are not, we find the story of exile and restoration turned into a personal prophecy, like a strange signpost standing in the mist, pointing ahead to the place where all the storylines of God, Israel, and the world converge.

In that context, too, we can see at last the multiplicity of ways in which the Israel of Jesus's own day was able to think and speak about the coming together of heaven and earth. We noticed in the previous chapter how the Temple functioned that way. The Glorious Presence of YHWH, dwelling in the tent, and then in the Temple itself, was referred to as "the tabernacling"—that is, the *Shekinah;* it was a way of the God of heaven being present on earth with and for his people. By Jesus's day similar ideas were being developed in relation to the Torah, God's gift to his redeemed people; if you kept the Torah, it was as though you were in the Temple itself—that is, at the place where heaven and earth met. We saw a moment ago another strand that points in the same direction: God's "word," the word by which all things are made, will go out once more to make all things new. Similar things could be said about God's "wisdom," an idea which begins, it seems, with the notion that when God made the world he did so wisely, and develops until "Wisdom" becomes a figure in her own right (*chokmah,* the word for "wisdom," is feminine in Hebrew, and so is s*ophia,* the Greek equivalent). "Wisdom" is then another vital way of speaking about God's action within the world, about the coming together of God's sphere and ours. Finally, going back once more to Genesis, God's powerful wind, his breath, his Spirit (all three are ways of translating the same original word) is let loose in the world to bring new life.

Presence, Torah, Word, Wisdom, and Spirit: five ways of saying the same thing. The God of Israel is the creator and redeemer of Israel and the world. In faithfulness to his ancient promises, he will act within Israel and the world to bring to its climax the great story of exile and restoration, of the divine rescue operation, of the king who brings justice, of the Temple that joins heaven and earth, of the Torah that binds God's people together, and of creation healed and restored. It is not only heaven and earth that are to come together. It is God's future and God's present.

It's a wonderful dream. Rich, multilayered, full of pathos and power. But why should anyone suppose that it—or anything else that might be built upon it—is anything more than a dream? Why should we imagine it's true?

The whole New Testament is written to answer that question. And the answers all focus, of course, on Jesus of Nazareth.

Seven

Jesus and the Coming of God's Kingdom

Christianity is about something that *happened*. Something that happened *to Jesus of Nazareth*. Something that happened *through* Jesus of Nazareth.

In other words, Christianity is *not* about a new moral teaching— as though we were morally clueless and in need of some fresh or clearer guidelines. This is not to deny that Jesus, and some of his first followers, gave some wonderfully bracing and intelligent moral teaching. It is merely to insist that we find teaching like that within a larger framework: the story of things that happened through which the world was changed.

Christianity isn't about Jesus offering a wonderful moral example, as though our principal need was to see what a life of utter love and devotion to God and to other people would look like, so that we could try to copy it. If that had been Jesus's main purpose, we could certainly say it had some effect. Some people's lives really have been changed simply by contemplating and imitating the example of Jesus. But observing Jesus's example could equally well simply make a person depressed. Watching Richter play the piano or Tiger Woods hit a golf ball doesn't inspire me to go out and copy them. It makes me realize that I can't come close and never will.

Nor is Christianity about Jesus offering, demonstrating, or even accomplishing a new route by which people can "go to heaven when they die." This is a persistent mistake, based on the medieval notion that the point of all religion—the rule of the game, if you like—was to make sure you ended up at the right side of the stage at the end of the mystery play (that is, in heaven rather than in hell), or on the right side of the painting in the Sistine Chapel. Again, that isn't to deny that our present beliefs and actions have lasting consequences. Rather, it's to deny both that Jesus made this the focus of his work and that this is the "point" of Christianity.

Finally, Christianity isn't about giving the world fresh teaching about God himself—though clearly, if the Christian claim is true, we do indeed learn a great deal about who God is by looking at Jesus. The need which the Christian faith answers is not so much that we are ignorant and need better information, but that we are lost and need someone to come and find us, stuck in the quicksand waiting to be rescued, dying and in need of new life.

So what *is* Christianity about, then?

Christianity is all about the belief that the living God, in fulfillment of his promises and as the climax of the story of Israel, has accomplished all this—the finding, the saving, the giving of new life—in Jesus. He has done it. With Jesus, God's rescue operation has been put into effect once and for all. A great door has swung open in the cosmos which can never again be shut. It's the door to the prison where we've been kept chained up. We are offered freedom: freedom to experience God's rescue for ourselves, to go through the open door and explore the new world to which we now have access. In particular, we are all invited—summoned, actually—to discover, through following Jesus, that this new world is indeed a place of justice, spirituality, relationship, and beauty, and that we are not only to enjoy it as such but to work at bringing it to birth on earth as in heaven. In listening to Jesus, we discover whose voice it is that has echoed around the hearts and minds of the human race all along.

What Can We Know About Jesus?

Writing about Jesus has been a growth industry for the last century or more. This is partly because he haunts the memory and imagination of Western culture like few (if any) other figures of either past or present. We still date our lives in reference to his supposed birth. (Actually, the sixth-century monk who did the calculation got it wrong by a few years; Jesus was probably born in or shortly before 4 BC, the year when Herod the Great died.) In my country, even those who know little or nothing about Jesus still use his name as a swearword, which is a kind of backhanded compliment to his ongoing cultural impact.

In America, wild claims about Jesus still make front-page news: perhaps he never did or said what the gospels say, perhaps he was married, perhaps he didn't think he was the Son of God, and so on. People write novels and other works of historical fiction whose plots turn on fantasyland interpretations of Jesus—for example, *The Da Vinci Code* by Dan Brown, which insists (among many other things) that Jesus married Mary Magdalene and fathered a child. The extraordinary popularity of this book can't be explained simply in terms of its being a cleverly written thriller. There are plenty of those. Something about Jesus, and the chance that there might be more to him than our culture has realized, still awakens in millions a sense of new possibilities and prospects.

Part of the reason for all this is that, like every figure of history, Jesus is open to reinterpretation. People write revisionist biographies of Winston Churchill, for whom we have truckloads of evidence; or of Alexander the Great, for whom we have considerably less. In fact, the more evidence you have, the more there is to interpret this way or that; the less evidence you have, the more you have to make educated guesses to fill in the blanks. Thus, whether we look at a recent figure for whom we have far too much information, or an ancient figure for whom we have far too little, the historian always has plenty of work to do.

Jesus has something of both, and more besides. We obviously have far less material about him than we do about, say, Churchill or John F. Kennedy. But we know a good deal more about Jesus than about most people in the ancient world—say, Tiberius, the Roman emperor when Jesus died, or Herod Antipas, the Jewish ruler at the same time. In fact, we have so many sayings attributed to Jesus, so many actions he is said to have performed, that we are spoiled for choice, and a short treatment like the present chapter and the next can only touch on a few of them.

But at the same time there are tantalizing gaps, not only for most of Jesus's early life but also in some of the things a contemporary biographer would want to know. Nobody tells us what Jesus looked like or what he ate for breakfast. Nobody, more important, tells us how he read the scriptures or—except for brief flashes—how he prayed. The trick, then, is so to understand Jesus's world—the complicated and dangerous world of the Middle East in the first century—that we can make historical, personal, and theological sense of what he was trying to do, what he believed he was called to accomplish.

There is, as I said, something more, something which makes the attempt to understand Jesus more complex and contested than the quest to understand any other figure of history, ancient or modern. Christians have claimed from the very beginning that, though Jesus is no longer walking around Palestine and available for us to meet him and get to know him in that sense, he is indeed "with us" in a different sense, and that we can indeed get to know him in a manner not wholly unlike the way we get to know other people.

This is because it has been central to Christian experience, not merely to Christian dogma, that in Jesus of Nazareth heaven and earth have come together once and for all. The place where God's space and our space intersect and interlock is no longer the Temple in Jerusalem. It is Jesus himself. The same cosmology which made sense of the claim about the Temple makes sense of this claim, too. We recall that "heaven," in Jewish and Christian thought, isn't miles away up in the sky, but is, so to speak, God's dimension of the cosmos. Thus, though Christians believe that Jesus is now "in heaven," he is present, accessible, and indeed active within our world. For anyone who believes this, and tries to live by it, writing the history of Jesus is far more complicated than simply documenting the life of a figure from the past. It is more like writing the biography of a friend who is still very much alive and still liable to surprise us.

Wouldn't it be simpler, then, to say that we should abandon the attempt to write about Jesus as though he were a historical figure, and write instead about the Jesus of our present experience? Many in our day have advocated that vigorously, not least because they are understandably fed up with some of the rubbish—it's not too strong a word—that has been written both by scholars and by popular writers. But it won't do. It is hard enough, even when studying the historical evidence with full seriousness, to avoid remaking Jesus in our own image. When we abandon history, the brakes are off and the portrait slides away into fantasy.

The nastiest of these fantasies was the attempt by some German theologians in the 1930s to invent a non-Jewish (indeed, an anti-Jewish) Jesus—an attempt which has some worrying similarities with more recent non-Jewish portraits of Jesus. One of the healthy signs in contemporary scholarship has been the determined attempt to understand Jesus afresh *within* the Judaism of his day. By itself, though, this still leaves several questions unanswered. Granted that Jesus was a first-century Jew, what *sort* of a first-century Jew was he? This at least puts us at the right point from which to begin.

Can We Trust the Gospels?

The key question for studying Jesus is: Can we trust the gospels? I am referring to the four books which are known by the names of Matthew, Mark, Luke, and John, and which are found in the "canon" of the New Testament—that is, the collection of books

that the church, from early on, recognized as authentic and authoritative (hence the often-used phrase "the canonical gospels"). There
has been a recent spate of books, both scholarly and popular, urging
us to think that these gospels were only four among dozens of similar works that were around in the early church, and that these four
were eventually privileged, and the others discarded, suppressed, or
even banned. The prime reason for adopting these four, it is sometimes suggested, was that they supported a view of Jesus which
was convenient for the ruling authorities at a time when, in the
fourth century, Christianity was becoming the official religion of
the Roman Empire.

Does this mean we have to tear up all the pictures of Jesus based
on the canonical gospels and start again? No. All kinds of other
documents have indeed turned up, not least a whole cache found
in Nag Hammadi in Upper Egypt in 1945, some of which give us
fascinating glimpses of what people were saying about Jesus at the
time of their writing. (The Dead Sea Scrolls, by the way—found
not long after the Nag Hammadi documents—say nothing whatever about Jesus or the early Christians, despite many ill-informed
assertions to the contrary.) But none of them, in fact, is able to
trump the gospels we already had.

Take the best known, and one of the longest, of the Nag Hammadi documents: a collection of supposed sayings of Jesus known
as the Gospel of Thomas. This is the book which, it has often been
suggested, could and should be treated as at least equal, and quite
possibly superior, to the canonical gospels as a historical source for
Jesus himself. The version of Thomas we now have, like most of
the Nag Hammadi material, is written in Coptic, a language spoken in Egypt at the time. But it has been demonstrated that Thomas is a translation from Syriac, a language quite like the Aramaic that
Jesus must have spoken (though he pretty certainly spoke Greek as
well, just as many people in today's world speak English as a second
language). But the Syriac traditions that Thomas embodies can be
dated, quite reliably, not to the first century at all, but to the second

half of the second century. That is over a hundred years after Jesus's own day—in other words, seventy to a hundred years after the time when the four canonical gospels were in widespread use across the early church.

What's more, despite efforts to prove the opposite, the sayings of Jesus as they appear in Thomas show clear indications that they are not as original as the parallel material (where it exists) in the canonical gospels. Sayings have, in many cases, been quietly doctored in Thomas to express a very different viewpoint. For instance, when Jesus says, in Matthew, Mark, and Luke, "Render to Caesar the things that are Caesar's, and to God the things that are God's," the saying in Thomas has an extra phrase at the end: ". . . and to me the things that are mine." What is going on here? In the worldview represented by Thomas, the word "God" denotes *a second-rate kind of deity who made the present wicked world,* the world from which Jesus has come to rescue people. Thomas and most of the other Nag Hammadi documents represent a worldview known as "Gnosticism," in which the present world is a dark, evil place from which we need to be rescued by "gnosis," a special knowledge of hidden truth—a world quite different from the Jewish world of Jesus and the four canonical gospels.

Thomas and the other works like it—that is, almost all the so-called "gospels" outside the New Testament—are collections of sayings. There is hardly any narrative about things Jesus did or things that happened to him. But the four canonical gospels are quite different. They are not mere collections of sayings. They tell a *story:* the story of Jesus himself, told as the climax of the story of Israel, told as the fulfillment of the promises of God, the creator, the covenant God of Abraham, Isaac, and Jacob. The Nag Hammadi and similar texts have broken away entirely from the world we have been studying in the previous two chapters of this book—the world in which, if Jesus really was a credible Jew of the early first century, he must have belonged. The four canonical gospels all insist on placing him there, though unfortunately the church's tradition of reading only small segments of scripture in worship has obscured this fact. Part of the reason for the historical study of Jesus and the gospels is that the church itself, let alone the world, needs reminding again and again of what the gospels are really talking about.

What is more, those four canonical gospels must all have been written by about AD 90 at the very latest. (I am inclined to think they are probably a lot earlier than that, but they cannot be later.) They are known and referred to by Christian writers in the first half of the second century, long before anyone begins to discuss the material we now know from Nag Hammadi. And they incorporate, and are based on, sources both oral and written which go back a lot earlier, sources from the time when not only most of Jesus's followers were still alive and active within the early Christian movement, but when plenty of others—bystanders, opponents, officials—were still around, aware of the new movement as it was growing, and ready to challenge or contradict tales that were gaining currency. Palestine is a small country. In a world without print and electronic media, people were eager to hear and eager to pass on stories about anyone and anything out of the ordinary. The chances are, as John suggests at the end of his gospel, that there was in fact far more material available about Jesus than any one of the gospel writers had space to put down. Source material must have been plentiful. The central features of Jesus's life and work must have been well known. As one of the early preachers says, these things were not done in a corner.

It is not as easy to reconstruct the sources of the gospels as has sometimes been imagined. In particular, I have never shared the enthusiasm for a source widely referred to as "Q," which many suppose lies behind Matthew and Luke. If such a source ever existed, it is tenuous in the extreme (though this hasn't stopped intrepid souls from making the attempt) first to reconstruct it and then to use that reconstruction as a measuring stick over against Matthew and Luke themselves. It is even shakier to suggest, as some have done in recent times, that such a source represents an entire strand of early Christianity, with its own beliefs and way of life. It is much more likely, in my judgment, that the gospel writers were able to draw on a bewildering variety of sources, many of them oral (in a world where oral reports were prized more highly than written ones), and many of them from eyewitnesses.

This doesn't mean, of course, that everything the gospels say is thereby automatically validated. Assessing their historical worth can be done, if at all, only by the kind of painstaking historical work which I and others have attempted at some length but for which there is no room in a book of the present kind. I simply record it as my conviction that the four canonical gospels, broadly speaking, present a portrait of Jesus of Nazareth which is firmly grounded in real history. As the late historian John Roberts, author of the monumental *History of the World* (1980), sums it up, "[the gospels] need not be rejected; much more inadequate evidence about far more intractable subjects has often to be employed [in writing history]." The portrait of Jesus we find in the canonical gospels makes sense within the world of Palestine in the 20s and 30s of the first century. Above all, it makes coherent sense in itself. The Jesus who emerges is thoroughly believable as a figure of history, even though the more we look at him, the more we feel once more that we may be staring into the sun.

The Kingdom of God

"The kingdom of God is at hand." This announcement was the center of Jesus's public proclamation. He was addressing the world we described at the end of the previous chapter, the world in which the Jewish people were anxious for their God to rescue them from pagan oppression and put the world to rights—in other words, to become king fully and finally. The gospels tell the story in such a way as to hold together the ancient promises and the urgent current context, with Jesus in the middle of it all. There is no good reason to doubt that this was how Jesus himself saw his own work.

But what did he mean? The prophet Isaiah, in line with several Psalms and other biblical passages, had spoken of God's coming kingdom as the time when (a) God's promises and purposes would be fulfilled, (b) Israel would be rescued from pagan oppression, (c) evil (particularly the evil of oppressive empires) would be judged, and (d) God would usher in a new reign of justice and peace. Daniel had envisaged a coming time when the monsters (that is, the pagan empires) would do their worst, and God would vindicate his people to set everything straight. The world was to be turned the right way up at last. To speak of God's kingdom arriving in the present was to summon up that entire narrative, and to declare that it was reaching its climax. God's future was breaking in to the present. Heaven was arriving on earth.

Jesus's message about God's kingdom wasn't the first time his contemporaries had heard language like that. Twice during Jesus's boyhood Jewish revolutionaries had urged their countrymen to resist Rome's imperial demand for a census and for consequent taxation. "There should be no king but God," they said; in other words, it's time for God's kingdom rather than these corrupt human ones. The Romans put down the rebellions with their usual cold, brutal thoroughness. The very phrase "God's kingdom" must have made many Jews of the time think at once of crucifixion, the standard death sentence for rebels. So what did Jesus mean when he went around telling people that God's kingdom was coming into being even as he spoke?

He believed that the ancient prophecies were being fulfilled. He believed that Israel's God was doing a new thing, renewing and reconstituting Israel in a radical way. His cousin John the Baptist, who had also announced God's coming kingdom and had told the people to get ready for someone else who was coming after him, had spoken in drastic terms of the ax being laid to the roots of the tree. God, he said, was quite capable of raising up children for Abraham from the stones lying on the ground.

If this was a rescue operation, it was one with a difference. It wasn't a matter of the God of Israel simply fighting off the wicked pagans and vindicating his own people. It was more devastating. It was about God judging not only the pagans but also Israel; about God acting in a new way in which nothing could be taken for granted; about God fulfilling his promises, but doing so in a way that nobody had expected or anticipated. God was issuing a fresh challenge to Israel, echoing back to his promises to Abraham: Israel is indeed the light of the world, but its present policies have been putting that light under a bucket. It's time for drastic action. Instead of the usual military revolt, it was time to show the pagans what the true God was really like, not by fighting and violence but by loving one's enemies, turning the other cheek, going the second mile. That is the challenge which Jesus issued in a series of teachings that we call the "sermon on the mount" (Matthew 5:1–7:29).

How do you get across a message as radical as that? How do you say something so drastic to people who are expecting something quite different? In two ways in particular: by symbols (particularly dramatic actions) and by stories. Jesus used both. His choice of twelve close followers ("disciples"—that is, "learners") was a powerful symbol in itself, speaking of the remaking of the whole people of God, the twelve tribes of Israel descended from the twelve sons of Jacob. That remaking of God's people was at the heart, too, of his remarkable healings. There is no doubt, historically, that he possessed healing powers; that was why he attracted not only crowds but also accusations of being in league with the devil.

But Jesus didn't see his healings simply as a kind of premodern traveling hospital. He wasn't healing the sick just for the sake of it, important though the healing itself was. Nor was it just a way of attracting people to listen to his message. Rather, the healing was a dramatic sign of the message itself. God, the world's creator, was at work through him, to do what he had promised, to open blind eyes and deaf ears, to rescue people, to turn everything right side up. The people who had been at the bottom of the heap would find themselves, to their own great surprise, on top. "Blessed are the meek," he said, "for they shall inherit the earth." And he went about making it happen.

Equally, he told stories—stories which got under the skin of his contemporaries precisely because they both were and were not the stories they were expecting. The ancient prophets had spoken about God replanting Israel after the long winter of exile; Jesus told stories about people sowing seed, about some seed being fruitful but a good deal going to waste, about seeds growing secretly and then a sudden harvest, about tiny seeds producing great shrubs. These "parables" weren't, as has often been supposed, "earthly stories with heavenly meanings." The whole point of Jesus's work was to bring heaven to earth and join them together forever, to bring God's future into the present and make it stick there. But when heaven comes to earth and finds earth unready, when God's future arrives in the present while people are still asleep, there will be explosions. And there were.

In particular, the people we would today call "the religious right," led by a popular though unofficial pressure group called the "Pharisees," objected strongly to Jesus's teaching that God's kingdom was coming in this way, through his own work. They were scandalized, not least by the way in which Jesus was celebrating God's kingdom—another strong symbol, this—*with all the wrong people:* the poor, the outcasts, the hated tax-collectors—anyone in fact who wanted to join in. It was in response to this criticism that Jesus told some of his most poignant and powerful parables.

Among these is a story often called "the parable of the prodigal son" (found in Luke 15). The younger of two sons leaves home, disgraces himself and his family, and then returns penitent to an astonishing welcome. The older son, who stays at home, bitterly resents the father's lavish welcome for the returning prodigal. There are long biblical echoes here—of Jacob and Esau, of exile and restoration. As with most of Jesus's parables, the story compels the hearers to put themselves in the picture and thereby discover the truth about Jesus—and about themselves. The parable is told to make a specific point: This is why there's a party going on with all the wrong people attending it; and this is what you look like if you're refusing to join in. God's kingdom is happening under your noses, and you can't see it. What's more, if you don't watch out, you will find yourself outside the door.

But it wasn't only the unofficial pressure groups, anxious (of course) about Israel's loyalty to the Torah and about the danger of Jesus teaching people things which didn't easily square with their tradition, who were concerned about Jesus's teaching. Kingdom-announcements, as we saw, meant rebellion, and the complicated power systems of the day couldn't avoid taking note. Herod Antipas (a pale shadow of his father, Herod the Great, but still powerful and malevolent) was officially "king of the Jews" at this time. He casts a shadow across the pages of the story. But in Jerusalem, the center of power, it was the chief priests, the guardians of the Temple itself, who actually ran things. Behind them all, operating through a governor who could call up reinforcements from nearby Syria, was the brooding power of Rome. When Jews of Jesus's day read Daniel's story about four sea-monsters coming to attack God's people, they interpreted it with Rome being the fourth and fiercest. It was time for God to act, to take his throne, to rescue his people, to bring in his kingdom, to put the world to rights. Jesus's kingdom-language must have stirred precisely those echoes.

So what did Jesus intend by it all? What did he think would happen next? Why did he walk into trouble in this way? And why, after his own violent death, did anyone take him seriously any longer, let alone suppose that he was the living embodiment of the one true God?

Eight

Jesus: Rescue and Renewal

Jesus had gone about Palestine announcing that now, at last, God's kingdom was arriving. The message went out as much by what he did as by what he said—the message, that is, that the ancient prophecies were coming true, that Israel's story was reaching its destination at last, that God himself was on the move once more and was about to rescue his people and put the world to rights.

So when Jesus began to tell his disciples that "the Son of Man must suffer many things, and be killed, and on the third day rise again" (Mark 8:31), we can be pretty certain that they would have understood his words as a coded reference, echoing biblical prophecies, to the coming kingdom of God, to God's future arriving in the present, bringing the fulfillment of all their long-cherished hopes. They must have supposed that Jesus was speaking, as so often, in riddles, in parables soaked in scripture and sharpened to a fine point. This time, though, they couldn't work out what he meant.

Hardly surprising, because they had come to regard him as Israel's Messiah, YHWH's anointed, the king-in-waiting for whom the nation had longed. "Messiah," remember, is a Hebrew or Aramaic word meaning "anointed"; when translated into Greek (the universal language of the day) it came out as "Christ." For the early

Christians, "Christ" wasn't just a name; it was a title with specific meaning.

Not all Jews of this period believed in or wanted a coming Messiah. But those who did, and they were many, cherished a frequently repeated set of expectations as to what the anointed one would do when he arrived. He would fight the battle against Israel's enemies—specifically, the Romans. He would rebuild, or at least cleanse and restore, the Temple (a task that, as noted earlier, the Herod family had undertaken, to press their claim to be the true royal house). He would bring Israel's long history to its climax, reestablishing the monarchy as in the days of David and Solomon. He would be God's representative to Israel, and Israel's representative to God.

All this can be seen both in various texts of the period and in some of the would-be Messiahs that flit through the pages of history. A hundred years after Jesus, Simeon ben Kosiba was hailed as Messiah by one of the greatest rabbis of the day, Akiba. Simeon minted coins with the year 1, then 2, and then 3, before his rebellion was crushed by the Romans. One of those coins carries a picture of the Temple, which was still in ruins after the disaster of AD 70. Central to Simeon's aim was to rebuild it, and thereby to place himself in the long line: David, Solomon, Hezekiah, Josiah, Judas Maccabaeus, Herod . . . all kings of the Jews, all Temple-builders or Temple-restorers. For that to happen, he would have to fight the ultimate battle against the pagan forces. Simeon's agenda fits the messianic pattern exactly.

So why did Jesus's followers hail him as Messiah? He had led no military uprising, nor did it look as though he would do so. (Some have tried to argue otherwise, but the case is hard to make.) He hadn't spoken of rebuilding the Temple. Indeed, he hadn't offered any explicit teaching about the Temple as part of his public proclamation. He had acted in powerful ways, collecting and holding crowds; but then, just when people were going to hail him as king, he had slipped away and escaped (John 6:15). Most people saw him as a prophet, and Jesus seems to have acted and spoken in such a way as to encourage that view. Nevertheless, his closest followers saw him as more than just a prophet, and he himself hinted at this when he spoke cryptically about his cousin John. One of the last biblical prophets had spoken of the prophet Elijah returning to prepare the world for the coming great day. After Elijah there was only one person left to come—namely, the Messiah himself. Jesus had suggested that John was Elijah. The implication was clear (Matthew 11:9–15).

But nobody in this period supposed that the Messiah would have to suffer, let alone die. Indeed, that was the very opposite of normal expectations. The Messiah was supposed to be leading the triumphant fight against Israel's enemies, not dying at their hands. This is why, having come to the view that their extraordinary leader was indeed God's anointed, the disciples couldn't imagine that he meant it literally when he spoke of his coming death and resurrection. Resurrection was something which, in Jewish belief, would happen to all God's people at the very end, not to one person in the middle of history.

Jesus appears to have seen it differently, and here we come close to the heart of his own understanding of his vocation. We have already noted—with unavoidable Christian hindsight—that at the heart of Isaiah's prophecy stood the figure of the "Suffering Servant," a development of royal ideas earlier in that Old Testament book. So far as we can tell from surviving sources, the Jews of Jesus's day understood this figure in two different ways. Some saw the Servant as a Messiah all right; but the "suffering" of which Isaiah spoke would be the suffering he would inflict on Israel's enemies. Others saw the Servant as one who would suffer; but this meant—inevitably, in their eyes—that he couldn't be the Messiah.

Jesus seems to have combined the two interpretations in a creative, indeed explosive, way. The Servant would be both royal and a sufferer. And the Servant would be . . . Jesus himself. Isaiah was by no means the only text upon which Jesus drew for his sense of vocation, which we must assume he had thrashed out in thought and prayer over some considerable time. But it is in Isaiah, particularly the central section, that we find that combination of themes— God's coming kingdom, the renewal of creation expressed not least in remarkable healings, the power of God's "word" to save and restore, the ultimate victory over all the "Babylons" of the world, and the figure of the Servant itself—which we find again so strikingly in the gospels. Like an optician putting several different lenses in front of our eyes until at last we can read the screen in front of us, we need to have all these themes and images in mind if we are to understand what Jesus believed he was called to do, and why.

Plenty of other Jews of Jesus's day studied the scriptures with care, insight, and attention. There is every reason to suppose that Jesus did the same, and that he allowed this study to shape his sense of what he had to do. His task, he believed, was to bring the great story of Israel to its decisive climax. The long-range plan of God the creator—to rescue the world from evil and to put everything to rights at last—was going to come true in him. His death, which at one level could rightly be seen as an enormous miscarriage of justice, would also be the moment when, as the prophet Isaiah had said, Jesus would be "wounded for our transgressions, and bruised for our iniquities" (Isaiah 53:5). God's plan to rescue the world from evil would be put into effect by evil doing its worst to the Servant—that is, to Jesus himself—and thereby exhausting its power.

Temple, Supper, and Cross

Matters came to a head when Jesus, with his disciples and a growing crowd, arrived in Jerusalem for one last Passover. The choice of festival was no accident. Jesus was as alive as anyone to the symbolic power of the ancient scriptural stories. His whole vision was for God to act in one final great "exodus," rescuing Israel and the world from the "Babylons" that had enslaved them, and leading

them to a new Promised Land, the new creation of which his healings had been advance signposts.

But, to the surprise of many in Jerusalem, on his arrival he directed his attack not at the Roman garrison, but at the Temple itself.
Declaring it corrupt (a point on which many of his Jewish contemporaries would have agreed), he performed one of his greatest symbolic actions, overturning tables and, for a short but potent time,
preventing the normal business (which was the continual offering of sacrifices). The flurry of arguments which followed indicates
well enough what he had in mind: this was no cleanup operation,
but a sign that the Temple itself was under divine judgment. Jesus
was challenging, in the name of Israel's God, the very place where
God was supposed to live and do business with his people. As with
most of his symbolic actions, Jesus backed this up with detailed
teaching that made the same point: God would destroy the city and
the Temple, and would vindicate not the Jewish nation as a whole,
but Jesus himself and his followers.

Jesus must have known the likely result, though he could still have
avoided arrest had he wanted to. Instead, as the festival approached,
he gathered his twelve disciples for a final meal, in all probability
some kind of a Passover meal, to which he gave a new and startling
symbolic interpretation.

All the Jewish festivals are packed full of meaning, and Passover
is the most meaningful of all. The festival involves a dramatic retell-
ing of the exodus story, reminding everybody of the time when the
pagan tyrant was overthrown, when Israel was set free, when God
acted powerfully to save his people. Celebrating Passover always
carries, to this day, the hope that God will do so again. Jesus's fresh
understanding of Passover, given in interpreted action rather than
abstract theory, spoke of that future arriving immediately in the
present. God was about to act to bring in the kingdom, but in a
way that none of Jesus's followers (despite his attempts to tell them)
had anticipated. He would fight the messianic battle—by losing
it. The real enemy, after all, was not Rome, but the powers of evil

that stood behind human arrogance and violence, powers of evil with which Israel's leaders had fatally colluded. It was time for the evil which had dogged Jesus's footsteps throughout his career—the shrieking maniacs, the conspiring Herodians, the carping Pharisees, the plotting chief priests, the betrayer among his own disciples, the whispering voices within his own soul—to gather into one great tidal wave of evil that would crash with full force over his head.

So he spoke of the Passover bread as his own body that would be given on behalf of his friends, as he went out to take on himself the weight of evil so that they wouldn't have to bear it themselves. He spoke of the Passover cup as containing his own blood. Like the sacrificial blood in the Temple, it would be poured out to establish the covenant—but this time the *new* covenant spoken of by the prophet Jeremiah. The time had now come when, at last, God would rescue his people, and the whole world, not from mere political enemies, but from evil itself, from the sin which had enslaved them. His death would do what the Temple, with its sacrificial system, had pointed toward but had never actually accomplished. In meeting the fate which was rushing toward him, *he* would be the place where heaven and earth met, as he hung suspended between the two. He would be the place where God's future arrived in the present, with the kingdom of God celebrating its triumph over the kingdoms of the world by refusing to join in their spiral of violence. He would love his enemies, turn the other cheek, go the second mile. He would act out, finally, his own interpretation of the ancient prophecies which spoke to him of a suffering Messiah.

The next few hours were tragic and brutal. Jesus wrestled in prayer in the Garden of Gethsemane, with the darkness which he felt caving in upon him while he waited for arrest. The chief priests did what one might have expected: carried out a quick, quasi-legal procedure—enough to frame a charge of seditious talk against the Temple and ultimately of blasphemy. This could be conveniently translated, for the benefit of the Roman governor, into a charge of

sedition against Rome. The Roman governor was weak and inde-
cisive; the priests, manipulative. Jesus went to his death on a charge
of which he was innocent—actual rebellion against Rome—but of
which most of his contemporaries were guilty, at least in intention. Barabbas, a rebel leader, went free in his stead. A centurion,
looking up at his thousandth victim, saw and heard something he
hadn't expected and muttered that maybe this man *was* God's Son
after all.

The meaning of the story is found in every detail, as well as in
the broad narrative. The pain and tears of all the years were met
together on Calvary. The sorrow of heaven joined with the anguish
of earth; the forgiving love stored up in God's future was poured
out into the present; the voices that echo in a million human hearts,
crying for justice, longing for spirituality, eager for relationship,
yearning for beauty, drew themselves together into a final scream
of desolation.

Nothing in all the history of paganism comes anywhere near
this combination of event, intention, and meaning. Nothing in
Judaism had prepared for it, except in puzzling, shadowy prophecy.
The death of Jesus of Nazareth as the king of the Jews, the bearer
of Israel's destiny, the fulfillment of God's promises to his people of
old, is either the most stupid, senseless waste and misunderstanding
the world has ever seen, or it is the fulcrum around which world
history turns.

Christianity is based on the belief that it was and is the latter.

The First Easter

Christians believe that on the third day after he was executed—
on Sunday, the first day of the week—Jesus of Nazareth was bodily raised from the dead, leaving an empty tomb behind him. That,
primarily, is why we also believe that Jesus's death was not a messy,
tragic accident, but the surprising victory of God over all the forces of evil.

It is extremely difficult to explain the rise of Christianity, as a historical phenomenon, without saying something solid about Jesus's resurrection. But before we get to that we should be clear about a couple of points.

First, we are talking here about resurrection, not resuscitation. Even if the Roman soldiers, seasoned professionals when it came to killing, had unaccountably allowed Jesus to be taken down from the cross alive, and even if, after a night of torture and flogging and a day of crucifixion, he had managed to survive and emerge from the tomb, there is no way he could have convinced anyone that he had come *through death and out the other side*. He would have had to be helped through, at best, a long, slow recuperation. Of one thing we can be sure: had that been what happened, nobody would ever have said that Jesus was the Messiah, that God's kingdom had arrived, that it was time for a mission to tell the world that Jesus was its rightful Lord.

One theory that went against this conclusion was very popular a few years ago, but is now widely discredited. Some sociologists suggested that the disciples had been suffering from "cognitive dissonance," the phenomenon whereby people who believe something strongly go on saying it all the more shrilly when faced with contrary evidence. Failing to take the negative signs on board, they go deeper and deeper into denial, sustaining their position the only way they can: by shouting louder and trying to persuade others to join them.

Whatever the likely occurrence of this in other circumstances, there is simply no chance of it being the right explanation for the emergence of the early church. Nobody was expecting anyone, least of all a Messiah, to rise from the dead. A crucified Messiah was a failed Messiah. When Simeon ben Kosiba was killed by the Romans in AD 135, nobody went around afterward saying he really was the Messiah after all, however much they had wanted to believe that he had been. God's kingdom was something that had to happen in real life, not in some fantasyland.

Nor was it the case, as some writers are fond of saying, that the idea of "resurrection" was found in religions all over the ancient Near East. Dying and rising "gods," yes—corn kings, fertility deities, and the like. But—even supposing Jesus's very Jewish followers knew any traditions like those pagan ones—nobody in those religions ever supposed it actually happened to individual humans. No. The best explanation by far for the rise of Christianity is that Jesus really did reappear, not as a battered, bleeding survivor, not as a ghost (the stories are very clear about that), but as a living, bodily human being.

But the body was somehow different. The gospel stories are, at this point, unlike anything before or since. As one leading scholar has put it, it seems that the gospel writers were trying to explain something for which they didn't have a precise vocabulary. Jesus's risen body had many of the same properties as an ordinary body (it could talk, eat and drink, be touched, and so on), but it had others, too. It could appear and disappear, and pass through locked doors. Nothing in Jewish literature or imagination had prepared people for a portrait like this. If the gospel writers had made something up to fit a preconceived notion, the one thing they would certainly have done is describe the risen Jesus shining like a star. According to Daniel 12:3 (a very influential passage in Jewish thought at the time), this was how the righteous would appear at the resurrection. But Jesus didn't. His body seems to have been transformed in a way for which there was neither precedent nor prophecy, and of which there remains no second example.

That kind of conclusion is always frustrating from a scientific point of view. Science, after all, rightly studies phenomena which can be repeated in laboratory conditions. But history doesn't. Historians study things that happened once and once only; even if there are partial parallels, each historical event is unique. And the historical argument is quite clear. To repeat: far and away the best explanation for why Christianity began after Jesus's violent death is that he really was bodily alive again three days later, in a transformed body.

I am not suggesting that this (or any other argument) can *force* anyone to believe that Jesus was raised from the dead. It is always open to anyone to say, "Well, I haven't got a better explanation for the rise of Christianity; but since I know dead people never rise and never could, there must be some other explanation." That is a perfectly logical position. The trouble is, of course, that believing that Jesus was raised from the dead involves, at the very least, suspending judgment on matters normally regarded as fixed and unalterable; or, to put it more positively, it requires that we exchange a worldview which says that such things can't happen for one which, embracing the notion of a creator God making himself known initially in the traditions of Israel and then fully and finally in Jesus, says that Jesus's resurrection makes perfect sense when seen from that point of view. Faith can't be forced, but unfaith can be challenged. That is how it has always been, from the very beginning, when people have borne witness to Jesus's resurrection.

There are, in fact, partial parallels to this kind of thing precisely in the world of contemporary science. Scientists now regularly ask us to believe things which seem strange and even illogical, not least in the areas of astrophysics or quantum mechanics. With something as basic as light, for example, they find themselves driven to speak in terms both of waves and of particles, though these appear incompatible. Sometimes, to make sense of the actual evidence before us, we have to pull our worldview, our sense of what's possible, into a new shape. That is the kind of thing demanded by the evidence about Easter.

But what does it all *mean*? Here recent generations of Western Christians have taken a drastic wrong turn. Faced with an increasingly secular world all around, and with denials that there is any life at all beyond the grave, many Christians have seized upon Jesus's resurrection as the sign that there really is "life after death." This tends to confuse things. Resurrection isn't a fancy way of saying "going to heaven when you die." It is not about "life after death" as such. Rather, it's a way of talking about being bodily alive again *after* a period of being bodily dead. Resurrection is a *second-stage* postmortem life: "life *after* 'life after death.'" If Jesus's resurrection "proves" anything about what happens to people after they die, it is that. But interestingly, none of the resurrection stories in the gospels or in the book titled Acts of the Apostles (more colloquially called simply Acts) speaks of the event proving that some kind of afterlife exists. They all say, instead: "If Jesus has been raised, that means that God's new world, God's kingdom, has indeed arrived; and that means we have a job to do. The world must hear what the God of Israel, the creator God, has achieved through his Messiah."

Some have gone further down the road to misunderstanding. They have tried to fit the events of Easter into a version of the view I outlined earlier as Option Two—that is, the view of God and the world according to which the two of them are normally poles apart. In this view, the God who is normally somewhere else, outside our world altogether, sometimes steps in and does dramatic things, which should (in this view) be seen as interventions into the ordinary course of events. That is what, for most people, words like "miracle" and "supernatural" mean today. An interpretation of Jesus's resurrection along those lines ("the greatest miracle") has then stirred up others to respond that that's all very well for Jesus, but what about everyone else? If God can do tricks like that, why didn't he step in and stop the Holocaust or Hiroshima?

The answer is that the resurrection of Jesus—and everything else about him, for that matter—simply doesn't fit within Option Two in any of its varieties. (Nor, for that matter, can Jesus be fitted into Option One, though I have seen occasional attempts to make him simply a new manifestation of "natural" processes.) If Easter makes any sense at all, it makes sense within something much more like the classic Jewish worldview I outlined as Option Three: heaven and earth are neither the same thing, nor a long way removed from one another, but they overlap and interlock mysteriously in a number of ways; and the God who made both heaven and earth is at work from within the world as well as from without, sharing the pain of the world—indeed, taking its full weight upon his own shoulders. From that point of view, as the Eastern Orthodox churches have always emphasized, when Jesus rose again God's whole new creation emerged from the tomb, introducing a world full of new potential and possibility. Indeed, precisely because part of that new possibility is for human beings themselves to be revived and renewed, the resurrection of Jesus doesn't leave us as passive, helpless spectators. We find ourselves lifted up, set on our feet, given new breath in our lungs, and commissioned to go and make new creation happen in the world.

That is, indeed, the interpretation of the resurrection which fits most closely the view of Jesus's life and work which I have presented. If it is the case that Israel's vocation was to be the people through whom the one God would rescue his beloved creation; if it is the case that Jesus believed himself, as God's Messiah, to be bearing Israel's vocation in himself; and if it really is true that in going to his death he took upon himself, and in some sense exhausted, the full weight of the world's evil—then clearly there is indeed a task waiting to be done. The music he wrote must now be performed. The early disciples saw this, and got on with it. When Jesus emerged from the tomb, justice, spirituality, relationship, and beauty rose with him. Something has happened in and through Jesus as a result of which the world is a different place, a place where heaven and earth have been joined forever. God's future has arrived in the present. Instead of mere echoes, we hear the voice itself: a voice which speaks of rescue from evil and death, and hence of new creation.

Jesus and "Divinity"

The earliest Christians, those who had followed Jesus during his short public career, had never imagined that a Messiah would be *divine*. Part of our difficulty here is that people use the word "Christ" either as though it were a mere proper name ("Jesus Christ") or as though it were, in itself, a "divine" title. In the same way, the phrase "Son of God" is often quoted as if it meant, without more ado, "the second person of the divine Trinity." It didn't—at least, until the early Christians began to give it a new meaning that pointed in that direction. At the time, it was simply another epithet for the Messiah. The Bible had spoken of the coming king as YHWH's adopted Son. A high rank for a human being, no doubt; but there was no thought of such a king being the very embodiment, or (to use the Latin word) *incarnation,* of Israel's God himself.

But from the earliest days of Christianity we find an astonishing shift, for which again nothing in Jewish traditions of the time had prepared Jesus's followers. They remained firmly within Jewish monotheism; and yet they said, from very early on, that Jesus was indeed divine. When they spoke about Jesus they used precisely those categories which Jews over the previous centuries had developed for speaking of the presence and action of the one true God in the world: Presence (as in the Temple), Torah, Word, Wisdom, and Spirit. They said that he was the unique embodiment of the one God of Israel; that at his name every knee would bow, in heaven and on earth and under the earth; that he was the one through whom all things were made, and through whom now all things were being remade; that he was the living, incarnate Word of God; that he had, so to speak, the godness of God stamped so deep upon his person that it ran right through him. The early Christians had no intention of departing from Jewish-style monotheism. They would have insisted that they were searching out its true meaning.

And they said all this, not three or four centuries later, after a long period of reflection and development, at a point when it might conceivably have been socially or politically desirable to say it. They said it within a single generation. And they said it even though it was shocking to the religious sensibilities of both Jews and pagans. Moreover, they said it even though it meant a direct political confrontation with the claims of Rome. Caesar, after all, was "son of God"; he was "lord of the world"; his kingdom was all-powerful, and it was at his name that every knee already had to bow. The earliest Christian evaluation of Jesus as the place where heaven and earth met, the replacement for the Temple, the embodiment of the living God, was about as socially provocative, as well as theologically innovative, as it could possibly have been.

And yet they said it. And, in saying it, they pondered and mused over those hints within what they remembered of Jesus himself where it appeared that he had already believed it of himself.

At this point, again, many Christians have taken a wrong turn. They have spoken of Jesus as being "aware," during his lifetime, of his "divinity"—aware in a sense that made him instantly, almost casually, the possessor of such knowledge about himself as would have made events like his agony in the Garden of Gethsemane quite inexplicable. What I have argued for elsewhere, not to diminish the full incarnation of Jesus but to explore its deepest dimension, is that Jesus was aware of a call, a vocation, to do and be what, according to the scriptures, only Israel's God gets to do and be. That, I believe, is what it means to speak about Jesus being both truly divine and truly human. And we realize, once we remind ourselves that humans were made in God's image, that this is not a category mistake, but the ultimate fulfillment of the purpose of creation itself.

That is why, when Jesus went to Jerusalem that last time, he told stories about a king (or a master) going away and eventually coming back to see how his subjects or servants were getting on. Jesus was speaking of YHWH himself, having left Israel at the time of the exile, coming back at last to judge and to save. But, though Jesus speaks of YHWH coming to Jerusalem, it is Jesus himself who is coming. It is Jesus, riding into the city on a donkey, assuming authority over the Temple, declaring to the high priest that he will be seated at the right hand of Power, giving his own flesh and blood for the sins of the world. The closer we get to the cross, the clearer the answer we get to the question, Who did Jesus think he was?

He must have known he might be mad. Jesus was certainly shrewd enough to be aware of the possibility of delusion. But—

and this is the most mysterious thing of all—he was sustained not only by his reading of scripture, in which he found so clearly the lines of his own vocation, but also by his intimate prayer life with the one he called *Abba,* Father. Somehow, Jesus *both* prayed to the Father *and* took upon himself a role which, in the ancient prophecies, was reserved for YHWH—that of rescuing Israel and the world. He was obedient to the Father, simultaneously doing what only God can do.

How can we make sense of this? I do not think that Jesus "knew he was divine" in the same way that we know we are cold or hot, happy or sad, male or female. It was more like the kind of "knowledge" we associate with vocation, where people *know,* in the very depths of their being, that they are called to be an artist, a mechanic, a philosopher. For Jesus, this seems to have been a deep "knowledge" of that kind, a powerful and all-consuming belief that Israel's God was more mysterious than most people had supposed; that within the very being of this God there was a give-and-take, a to-and-fro, a love given and received. Jesus seems to have believed that he, the fully human prophet from Nazareth, was one of those partners in love. He was called, in obedience to the Father, to follow through the project to which that love would give itself freely and fully.

This has brought us to the borders of language as well as theology. But the conclusion I have reached as a historian is that such an analysis best explains why Jesus did what he did, and why his followers, so soon after his death and resurrection, came to believe and do what they believed and did. And the conclusion I reach as a Christian is that this understanding of Jesus and his role explains, in turn, why it is that I and millions of others have discovered Jesus to be personally present and active in the world and in our lives, our rescuer and our Lord.

Nine

God's Breath of Life

I have just thrown open the window on a glorious spring morning. A fresh breeze is stirring around the garden. In the distance there is a crackle of bonfire as a farmer clears away some winter rubbish. Near the path down to the sea, a skylark is hovering over its nest. All around, there is a sense of creation throwing off its wintry coverings and getting ready for an outburst of new life.

All these (I didn't make them up, by the way) are images the early Christians used to describe something just as strange as the story of Jesus, but just as real in their own lives. They spoke of a powerful wind rushing through the house and entering them. They spoke of tongues of fire resting on them and transforming them. They picked up, from the ancient creation story, the image of a bird brooding over the waters of chaos, bringing to birth a new world of order and life.

How else can we explain the inexplicable, except in a rush of images from the world we already know?

There was something to explain, all right. Jesus's followers were clearly as puzzled by his resurrection as they had been by much of what he had been saying to them. They were unsure what they were supposed to do next. They were unclear what *God* was going to do next. At one point, they went back to their fishing. At another point—the last time they saw Jesus before he disappeared from sight for the last time—they asked him yet again whether all these strange goings-on meant that the old dream of Israel was going to come true after all. Was this the time, they asked, when Israel would receive the kingdom, would be free at last in the sense that they and their contemporaries had been hoping for?

As was so often the case, Jesus didn't answer their question directly. Many of the questions we ask God *can't* be answered directly, not because God doesn't know the answers but because our questions don't make sense. As C. S. Lewis once pointed out, many of our questions are, from God's point of view, rather like someone asking, "Is yellow square or round?" or "How many hours are there in a mile?" Jesus gently puts off the question. "It isn't for you," he says, "to know the times and periods which the Father has set by his own authority. But you will receive power when the Holy Spirit has come upon you; and you will be my witnesses in Jerusalem, in all Judaea and Samaria, and to the ends of the earth" (Acts 1:6–8).

The Holy Spirit and the task of the church. The two walk together, hand in hand. We can't talk about them apart. Despite what you might think from some excitement in the previous generation about new spiritual experiences, God doesn't give people the Holy Spirit in order to let them enjoy the spiritual equivalent of a day at Disneyland. Of course, if you're downcast and gloomy, the fresh wind of God's Spirit can and often does give you a new perspective on everything, and above all grants a sense of God's presence, love, comfort, and even joy. But the point of the Spirit is to enable those who follow Jesus to take into all the world the news that he is Lord, that he has won the victory over the forces of evil, that a new world has opened up, and that we are to help make it happen.

Equally, the task of the church can't be attempted without the Spirit. I have sometimes heard Christian people talk as though God, having done what he's done in Jesus, now wants us to do our part by getting on with things under our own steam. But that is a tragic misunderstanding. It leads to arrogance, burnout, or both. Without God's Spirit, there is nothing we can do that will count for God's kingdom. Without God's Spirit, the church simply can't be the church.

I use the word "church" here with a somewhat heavy heart. I know that for many of my readers that very word will carry the overtones of large, dark buildings, pompous religious pronouncements, false solemnity, and rank hypocrisy. But there is no easy alternative. I, too, feel the weight of that negative image. I battle with it professionally all the time.

But there is another side to it, a side which shows all the signs of the wind and fire, of the bird brooding over the waters and bringing new life. For many, "church" means just the opposite of that negative image. It's a place of welcome and laughter, of healing and hope, of friends and family and justice and new life. It's where the homeless drop in for a bowl of soup and the elderly stop by for a chat. It's where one group is working to help drug addicts and another is campaigning for global justice. It's where you'll find people learning to pray, coming to faith, struggling with temptation, finding new purpose, and getting in touch with a new power to carry that purpose out. It's where people bring their own small faith and discover, in getting together with others to worship the one true God, that the whole becomes greater than the sum of its parts. No church is like this all the time. But a remarkable number of churches are partly like that for quite a lot of the time.

Nor must we forget that it was the church in South Africa which worked and prayed and suffered and struggled so that, when major change happened and apartheid was overthrown and a new freedom came to that land, it came without the massive bloodshed we were all expecting. It was the church which stayed alive at the heart of the old Communist eastern Europe, and which at the end, with processions of candles and crosses, made it clear that enough was enough. It is the church which, despite all its follies and failings, is there when it counts in hospitals, schools, prisons, and many other places. I would rather rehabilitate the word "church" than beat about the bush with long-winded phrases like "the family of

God's people" or "all those who believe in and follow Jesus" or "the company of those who, in the power of the Spirit, are bringing God's new creation to birth." But I mean all those things when I say "church."

The wind and the fire and the brooding bird are given to enable the church to *be* the church—in other words, to enable God's people to *be* God's people. This has a surprising and dramatic effect. The Spirit is given so that we ordinary mortals can become, in a measure, what Jesus himself was: part of God's future arriving in the present; a place where heaven and earth meet; the means of God's kingdom going ahead. The Spirit is given, in fact, so that the church can share in the life and continuing work of Jesus himself, now that he has gone into God's dimension—that is, heaven. (The "ascension" is about just that: Jesus going ahead into God's sphere, against the day when heaven and earth become one and he is once again personally present in the new, combined, heaven-and-earth.)

Each of these points deserves to be explored a little further.

God's Spirit and God's Future

The Spirit is given to begin the work of making God's future real in the present. That is the first, and perhaps the most important, point to grasp about the work of this strange personal power for which so many images are used. Just as the resurrection of Jesus opened up the unexpected world of God's new creation, so the Spirit comes to us from that new world, the world waiting to be born, the world in which, according to the old prophets, peace and justice will flourish and the wolf and the lamb will lie down side by side. One key element of living as a Christian is learning to live with the life, and by the rules, of God's future world, even as we are continuing to live within the present one (which Paul calls "the present evil age" and Jesus calls "this corrupt and sinful generation").

That is why St. Paul, our earliest Christian writer, speaks of the Spirit as the *guarantee* or the *down-payment* of what is to come. The Greek word he uses is *arrabōn,* which in modern Greek means an engagement ring, a sign in the present of what is to come in the future.

Paul speaks of the Spirit as the guarantee of our "inheritance" (Ephesians 1:14). He isn't simply using an image taken from the ordinary human transaction whereby, when a person dies, someone else inherits his or her wealth—an "inheritance" from which one might perhaps receive something in advance, an early first installment. Nor is he simply speaking, as many Christians have supposed, of our "going to heaven," as though celestial bliss were the full "inheritance" God had in mind for us. No. He is drawing on a major biblical theme and taking it in a striking new direction. To grasp this is to see why the Spirit is given in the first place, and indeed who the Spirit actually is.

The theme upon which Paul is drawing when he speaks of the "inheritance" to come, of which the Spirit is given as a down payment, is our old friend the exodus story, in which Israel escapes from Egypt and goes off to the Promised Land. Canaan, the land we now call the Holy Land, was their promised "inheritance," the place where they would live as God's people. It was where—provided they maintained their side of the covenantal agreement—God would live with them and they with God. As both the foretaste of that promise, and the means by which they were led to inherit it, God went with them on the way, a strange holy Presence guiding and directing their wanderings and grieving over their rebellions.

So when Paul speaks of the Spirit as the "guarantee of our inheritance," he is evoking, as Jesus himself had done, this whole exodus tradition, the story which began with Passover and ended with the Promised Land. He is saying, in effect, You are now the people of the true exodus. You are now on your way to your inheritance.

But if that "inheritance" isn't a disembodied heaven, neither is it simply one small country among others. *The whole world is now*

God's holy land. At the moment the world appears as a place of suffering and sorrow as well as of power and beauty. But God is reclaiming it. That's what Jesus's death and resurrection were all about. And we are called to be part of that reclaiming. One day all creation will be rescued from slavery, from the corruption, decay, and death which deface its beauty, destroy its relationships, remove the sense of God's presence from it, and make it a place of injustice, violence, and brutality. That is the message of rescue, of "salvation," at the heart of one of the greatest chapters Paul ever wrote, the eighth chapter of his Letter to the Romans.

So what does it mean to say that this future has begun to arrive in the present? What Paul means is that those who follow Jesus, those who find themselves believing that he is the world's true Lord, that he rose from the dead—these people are given the Spirit as a foretaste of what that new world will be like. If anyone is "in the Messiah" (one of Paul's favorite ways of describing those who belong to Jesus), what they have and are is . . . new creation (2 Corinthians 5:17)! Your own human self, your personality, your body, is being reclaimed, so that instead of being simply part of the old creation, a place of sorrow and injustice and ultimately the shame of death itself, you can be both part of the new creation in advance and someone through whom it begins to happen here and now.

What does this say about the Holy Spirit? It says that the Spirit plays the same role in our pilgrimage from Passover to the Promised Land—from Jesus's resurrection, in other words, to the final moment when all creation will be renewed—that was played in the old story by the pillar of cloud and fire. The Spirit is the strange, personal presence of the living God himself, leading, guiding, warning, rebuking, grieving over our failings, and celebrating our small steps toward the true inheritance.

But if the Spirit is the personal presence of God himself, what does this say about us as Christians? Let Paul again give the answer. You, he says, are the Temple of the living God.

God's Spirit Between Heaven and Earth

If the Spirit is the one who brings God's future into the present, the Spirit is also the one who joins heaven and earth together. We are back again with Option Three. We had better remind ourselves how this works.

Option One, you'll recall, is to see heaven and earth as basically coterminous. It is a way of saying that there is a divine power, force, or presence in and with all that exists, ourselves included. This is pantheism. It is a way of recognizing that nothing in the world we know is free from the smell of divinity—but it goes on to conclude that that's *all* there is, that divinity is simply the sum total of this divine flavor we find in the earth, the rivers, the animals, the stars, and ourselves. Pan*en*theism allows that there is more to God than this but still has all of creation permeated with God's presence.

Within that scheme, speaking of God's Spirit at work within us appears easy. Of course, thinks the pantheist: if something we call "God" is within everything, talking of God's Spirit is just another way of saying the same thing. This seems fine and, in our modern world, "democratic." We don't like to think that God would be more particularly in and with some people or places than others; it offends our post-Enlightenment Western sensibilities.

I well remember the first pantheist I ever encountered, a girl I met while hitchhiking half the length of British Columbia in the summer of 1968. "Of course Jesus is divine," she said. (I can't remember how the conversation started, but she must have discovered that I was a Christian.) "But so am I. So are you. So is my pet rabbit."

Now I have nothing against pet rabbits (except that their owners, in my household, used to leave other people—namely, me—to clear out their hutches). But—and this, no doubt, is why the conversation stuck in my mind—to say that God's Spirit is in and with a pet rabbit *in the same sense* that God's Spirit was in and with Jesus struck me (and still strikes me) as absurd. That's the trouble with pantheism. It leaves you where you are. You already have all that there is. Not only is there no solution to evil; there is no future beyond where we now are. If Option One is true, Jesus was indeed a deluded fanatic.

Option Two might seem at first sight a better prospect for understanding the idea of God's fresh, fiery rushing wind. It suggests that God's sphere and ours are utterly different places. How wonderful, how exciting, how dramatic, to think of a power coming all the way from God's distant world to ours—to us—to me! This is where the language about "natural" and "supernatural" has played a key role for many people in our world. They suppose that everything in our sphere is "natural," to be explained by the ordinary laws of nature, physics, history, and so on, and that everything in God's sphere is "supernatural," entirely "other," completely unlike our ordinary experience. (I know that the words "natural" and "supernatural" have a longer and more interesting history than this last sentence might imply, but I'm talking about the way in which the words are commonly used today.) That is why people who have assumed a worldview something like Option Two have looked for evidence of the Holy Spirit's presence and work, not in a quiet growth of moral wisdom, a steady, undramatic lifetime of selfless service, but in spectacular "supernatural" events such as healings, speaking in tongues, wonderful conversions, and so on.

Please note: I am *not* saying that healings and speaking in tongues don't happen, or don't matter. They do, and they do. I'm not saying that God doesn't sometimes convert people with wonderful, dramatic suddenness. He does. What I *am* saying is that Option Two sets up the wrong framework for understanding what is going on. In particular, it excludes that sense of God's presence and power which already exists within the "natural" world.

Neither of the first two options will do as a framework for understanding what the New Testament says about the Spirit. For that, we need Option Three. Somehow, God's dimension and our dimension—heaven and earth—overlap and interlock. All the questions we want to ask—how does this happen, who does it happen to, when, where, why, under what conditions, what does it look like when it does?—remain partly mysterious, and will do so until creation is finally renewed and the two dimensions are joined into one as they were designed to be (and as Christians pray daily that they will be). But the point of talking about the Spirit within Option Three ought by now to be clear. If it wasn't, St. Paul would rub our noses in it: those in whom the Spirit comes to live are God's new Temple. They are, individually and corporately, places where heaven and earth meet.

Most of the next section of this book will be devoted to exploring and explaining what this means in practice. But one or two things must be said right away.

First, the obvious retort. "It doesn't look like that to me!" Most of us, thinking even of those Christians to whom we look up as examples, find it difficult to imagine that those people are walking Temples, places where heaven and earth meet. Most of us have even more difficulty thinking of *ourselves* in that way. We certainly find it hard, looking at all the tragic nonsense that has marred the history of Christianity, to see the church as a whole in this light.

But the counter-retort is equally obvious to anyone who knows the writings of St. Paul. *He could see the failings of the church, and of individual Christians, just as clearly as we can.* And it's in one of the letters where those failings are most embarrassingly obvious—Paul's first letter to the Christians in Corinth—where he makes the claim. You corporately, he says to the whole church, are God's Temple, and God's Spirit dwells within you (1 Corinthians 3:16). That's why the unity of the church matters so much. Your bodies, he says to them one by one, are Temples of the Holy Spirit within you (6:19). That's why bodily holiness, including sexual holiness, matters so much. Unity and holiness have been two great problems for the church in the last generation. Could it be that we need to recapture Paul's bracing teaching about the Holy Spirit?

✝

Ten

Living by the Spirit

Once we glimpse this vision of the Holy Spirit coming to live within human beings, making them Temples of the living God—which ought to make us shiver in our shoes—we are able to grasp the point of the Spirit's work in several other ways as well.

To begin with, building on the startling call to holiness we just noticed, we see right across the early Christian writings the notion that those who follow Jesus are called to fulfill the Law—that is, the Torah, the Jewish Law. Paul says it; James says it; Jesus himself says it. Now there are all kinds of senses in which Christians do *not*, and are not meant to, perform the Jewish Law. The New Testament Letter to the Hebrews insists that with the death of Jesus the sacrificial system came to an end, and with it the whole point of the Temple. Paul insists that when pagan men and boys believe the gospel of Jesus and get baptized, they do *not* have to get circumcised. Jesus himself hinted strongly that the food laws which had marked out the Jews from their pagan neighbors were to be set aside in favor of a different kind of marking out, a different kind of holiness. The early Christians, following Jesus himself, were quite clear that keeping the Jewish Sabbath was no longer mandatory, even though doing so was one of the Ten Commandments.

Nevertheless, the early Christians continued to speak, not least in the passages where they talked of the Spirit, of the obligation to fulfill the Law. If you are guided and energized by the Spirit, declares Paul, you will no longer do those things which the Law forbids—murder, adultery, and the rest. "The mind set on the flesh is hostile to God's Law," he writes in the Letter to the Romans. "Such a mindset does not submit to God's Law, indeed it can't; and those of that sort cannot please God." But, as he goes on at once, "You are not in the flesh, but in the Spirit, if God's Spirit does indeed dwell in you" (note the Temple language again). The Spirit will give life—resurrection life—to all those in whom the Spirit dwells; and this is to be anticipated (future-in-the-present language again) in holiness of life here and now (Romans 8:7–17). Later in the same letter, he explains further: "Love does no wrong to a neighbor; therefore love is the fulfilling of the Law" (13:10).

The point, once again, is not that the Law is a convenient moral guide, ancient and venerable. It is that the Torah, like the Temple, *is one of the places where heaven and earth meet,* so that, as some Jewish teachers had suggested, those who study and keep the Torah are like those who worship in the Temple. And the early Christians are encouraging one another to live as points of intersection, points of overlap, between heaven and earth. Again, this sounds fearsomely difficult, not to say downright impossible. But there is no getting around it. Fortunately, as we shall see, what ought to be normal Christianity is actually all about finding out how to sustain this kind of life and even grow in it.

The fulfillment of the Torah by the Spirit is one of the main themes underlying the spectacular description, in Acts 2, of the day of Pentecost itself. To this day, Pentecost is observed in Judaism as the feast of the giving of the Law. First comes Passover, the day when the Israelites leave their Egyptian slavery behind for good. Off they go through the desert, and fifty days later they reach Mount Sinai. Moses goes up the mountain and comes down with the Law, the tablets of the covenant, God's gift to his people of the way of life by which they will be able to demonstrate that they really are his people.

This is the picture we ought to have in mind as we read Acts 2. The previous Passover, Jesus had died and been raised, opening the way out of slavery, the way to forgiveness and a new start for the whole world—especially for all those who follow him. Now, fifty days later, Jesus has been taken into "heaven," into God's dimension of reality; but, like Moses, he comes down again, to ratify the renewed covenant and to provide the way of life, written not on stone but in human hearts, by which Jesus's followers may gratefully demonstrate that they really are his people. That is the underlying theology by which the remarkable phenomenon of Pentecost as Luke tells it—the wind, the fire, the tongues, and the sudden, powerful proclamation of Jesus to the astonished crowds—is given its deepest meaning. Those in whom the Spirit comes to dwell are to be people who live at the intersection between heaven and earth.

Nor is it only Temple and Torah that are fulfilled by the Spirit. Remember the two additional ways in which, in the language of ancient Judaism, God was at work within the world: God's word and God's wisdom.

Spirit, Word, and Wisdom

As the early Christians reflected on what God had done in Jesus, and on what God was doing in their own life and work by his Spirit, these two themes of God's word and God's wisdom played a vital role in their understanding.

When the first disciples were sent off by Jesus into the wider world to announce that he was Israel's Messiah and hence the world's true Lord, they knew that their message would make little or no sense to most of their hearers. It was an affront to Jewish people to tell them that Israel's Messiah had arrived—and that the Romans had crucified him at least in part because the Jewish leaders hadn't wanted to accept him! It was sheer madness, something to provoke sniggers or worse, to tell non-Jews that there was a single true God who was calling the whole world to account through a man whom he had sent and whom he had raised from the dead. And yet the early Christians discovered that telling this story carried a power which they regularly associated with the Spirit, but which they often referred to simply as "the word." Note these references from Acts: "Filled with the Holy Spirit, they spoke God's word with boldness." "The word of God continued to spread." "The word of God continued to advance and gain adherents." "The word of God grew mightily and prevailed" (Acts 4:31; 6:7; 12:24; 19:20).

Paul spoke this way, too. "When you received the word of God from us," he wrote, "you accepted it not as a human word, but as what it really is, God's word, which is also at work in you believers." This is "the word of truth, the gospel which has come to you . . . bearing fruit and growing in the whole world" (1 Thessalonians 2:13; Colossians 1:5–6). This last passage gives us another hint that the word is old as well as new: the phrase "bearing fruit and growing" is a direct allusion to the language of the first creation, of Genesis 1. "By the word of YHWH were the heavens made," sang the Psalmist, "and all the host of them by the breath of his mouth" (Psalm 33:6). Yes, replied the early Christians, and this same word is now at work through the good news, the "gospel," the message that declares Jesus as the risen Lord. "The word is near you, on your lips and in your heart; because if you confess with your lips that Jesus is Lord, and believe in your heart that God raised him from the dead, you will be saved" (Romans 10:8–9). In other words, when you announce the good news that the risen Jesus is Lord, that very word is the word of God, a carrier or agent of God's Spirit, a means by which, as Isaiah had predicted, new life from God's dimension comes to bring new creation within ours (Isaiah 40:8; 55:10–13).

So, finally, with wisdom as well. Wisdom (personified) was already thought of within Judaism as God's agent in creation, the one through whom the world was made. John, Paul, and the Letter to the Hebrews all draw on this idea to speak of Jesus himself as the one through whom God made the world. But it doesn't stop there. Paul, like the book of Proverbs, goes on to speak of this wisdom (no longer personified) being accessible to humans through the power of God's Spirit. As in Proverbs, part of the point about wisdom is that it's what you need in order to live a fully, genuinely human life. It is not, he says, a wisdom "of this age"—that is, of the present world and the way this world sees things. It doesn't conform to the kind of wisdom the rulers of the present world like to acknowledge. Instead, "we speak God's wisdom, secret and hidden, which God decreed before the ages for our glory" (1 Corinthians 2:7). God has given us access to a new kind of wisdom, through the Spirit.

All God's treasures of wisdom and knowledge are hidden in the Messiah himself. This means that those who belong to the Messiah have this wisdom accessible to them, and hence the chance to grow toward mature human and Christian living: "It is he whom we proclaim, warning everyone and teaching everyone in all wisdom, so that we may present everyone mature in the Messiah" (Colossians 1:28; 2:2–3). At this point, too, those in whom the Spirit dwells are called to be people who live at, and by, the intersection of heaven and earth.

Please note: only those who subscribe to Option Two could ever think of someone being "so heavenly minded that they are of no earthly use." For Option Three, the way to be truly of use on this earth is to be genuinely heavenly minded—and to live as one of the places where, and the means by which, heaven and earth overlap.

That's how the church is to carry forward the work of Jesus. The book of Acts says that in the previous book (referring back to the author's earlier volume—that is, the Gospel of Luke) the writer had described "all that Jesus *began* to do and teach." The implication is clear: that the story of the church, led and energized by the power of the Spirit, is the story of Jesus continuing to do and to teach— through his Spirit-led people. Once more, that's why we pray that God's kingdom will come, and his will will be done, "on earth as it is in heaven."

Toward Christian Spirituality

According to Christian belief, God's own Spirit offers the answer to the four questions with which this book began—questions about our yearnings for beauty, relationship, spirituality, and justice. We take them in reverse order.

God has promised that, through his Spirit, he will remake the creation so that it becomes what it is straining and yearning to be. All the beauty of the present world will be enhanced, ennobled, set free from that which at present corrupts and defaces it. Then there will appear that greater beauty for which the beauty we already know is simply an advance signpost.

God offers us, by the Spirit, a fresh kind of relationship with himself—and, at the same time, a fresh kind of relationship with our neighbors and with the whole of creation. The renewal of human lives by the Spirit provides the energy through which damaged and fractured human relationships can be mended and healed.

God offers us, through the Spirit, the gift of being at last what we know in our bones we were meant to be: creatures that live in both dimensions of his created order. The quest for spirituality now appears as a search for that coming together of heaven and earth which, deeply challenging though of course it is, is genuinely on offer to those who believe.

Finally, God wants to anticipate now, by the Spirit, a world set right, a world in which the good and joyful gift of justice has flooded creation. The work of the Spirit in the lives of individuals in the present time is designed to be another advance sign, a down payment and guarantee, as it were, of that eventual setting-right of all things. We are "justified" in the present (I'll say more about that later) in order to bring God's justice to the world, against the day when—still by the operation of the Spirit—the earth is filled with the knowledge of YHWH as the waters cover the sea.

Within this remarkable picture, two things stand out about characteristically Christian spirituality.

First, Christian spirituality combines a sense of the awe and majesty of God with a sense of his intimate presence. This is hard to describe but easy to experience. As Jesus addressed God by the Aramaic family word *Abba,* Father, so Christians are encouraged to do the same: to come to know God in the way in which, in the best sort of family, the child knows the parent. From time to time I have met Christians who look puzzled at this, and say that they have no idea what all that stuff is about. I have to say that being a Christian without having at least something of that intimate knowledge of the God who is at the same time majestic, awesome, and holy sounds like a contradiction in terms. I freely grant that there may be conditions under which, because of wounds in the personality, or some special calling of God, or some other reason, people may genuinely believe in the gospel of Jesus, strive to live by the Spirit, and yet have no sense of God's intimate presence. There is, after all, such a thing as the "dark night of the soul," reported by some who have probed the mysteries of prayer further than most of us. But Jesus declares that the Holy Spirit will not be denied to those who ask (Luke 11:13). One of the characteristic signs of the Spirit's work is precisely that sense of the intimate presence of God.

Second, Christian spirituality normally involves a measure of suffering. One of the times when Jesus is recorded as having used the *Abba*-prayer was when, in Gethsemane, he asked his Father if there was another way, if he really had to go through the horrible fate that lay in store for him. The answer was yes, he did. But if Jesus prayed like that, we can be sure that we will often have to as well. Both Paul and John lay great stress on this. Those who follow Jesus are called to live by the rules of the new world rather than the old one, and the old one won't like it. Although the life of heaven is designed to bring healing to the life of earth, the powers that presently run this earth have carved it up to their own advantage, and they resent any suggestion of a different way. That is why the powers—whether they are in politics or the media, in the professions or the business world—bitterly resent any suggestion from Christian leaders as to how things ought to be, even while sneering at the church for not "speaking out" on issues of the day.

Suffering may, then, take the form of actual persecution. Even in the liberal modern Western world—perhaps precisely in that world!—people can suffer discrimination because of their commitment to Jesus Christ. How much more so, in places where the worldview of those in power is explicitly stated to be opposed to the Christian faith in all its forms, as in some (not all) Muslim countries today. But suffering comes in many other forms, too: illness, depression, bereavement, moral dilemmas, poverty, tragedy, accidents, and death. Nobody reading the New Testament or any of the other Christian literature from the first two or three centuries could have accused the early Christians of painting too rosy a picture of what life would be like for those who follow Jesus. But the point is this: it is precisely when we are suffering that we can most confidently expect the Spirit to be with us. We don't seek, or court, suffering or martyrdom. But if and when it comes, in whatever guise, we know that, as Paul says toward the end of his great Spirit-chapter, "in all these things we are more than conquerors through him who loved us" (Romans 8:37).

Glimpsing the Triune God

How, then, can we summarize the Christian understanding of God? What does it mean, theologically speaking, to learn to stare at the sun?

God is the creator and lover of the world. Jesus spoke of God as "the Father who sent me," indicating that, as he says elsewhere, "anyone who has seen me has seen the Father" (John 14:9). Look hard at Jesus, especially as he goes to his death, and you will discover more about God than you could ever have guessed from studying the infinite shining heavens or the moral law within your own conscience. God is the one who satisfies the passion for justice, the longing for spirituality, the hunger for relationship, the yearning for beauty.

And God, the true God, is the God we see in Jesus of Nazareth, Israel's Messiah, the world's true Lord. The earliest Christians spoke of God and Jesus in the same breath and, so to speak, on the same side of the equation. When Paul quoted the most famous slogan of Jewish monotheism ("Hear, O Israel; YHWH our God, YHWH is One"), he explained "the Lord"—that is, YHWH—in terms of Jesus, and "God" in terms of "the Father": "For us," he wrote, "there is one God (the Father, from whom are all things and we to him), and one Lord (Jesus the Messiah, through whom are all things and we through him)" (1 Corinthians 8:6). Even earlier, he had written that if you want to know who the real God is, as opposed to the non-gods of paganism, you must think in terms of the God who, to fulfill his age-old plan to rescue the world, sent first his Son and then the Spirit of his Son (Galatians 4:4–7).

The church's official "doctrine of the Trinity" wasn't fully formulated until three or four centuries after the time of Paul. Yet when the later theologians eventually worked it all through, it turned out to consist, in effect, of detailed footnotes to Paul, John, Hebrews, and the other New Testament books, with explanations designed to help later generations grasp what was already there in principle in the earliest writings.

But it would be a mistake to give the impression that the Christian doctrine of God is a matter of clever intellectual word games or mind games. For Christians it's always a love game: God's love for the world calling out an answering love from us, enabling us to discover that God not only happens to love us (as though this was simply one aspect of his character) but that he *is* love itself. That's what many theological traditions have explored as the very heart of God's own being, the love which passes continually between Father, Son, and Spirit. Indeed, some have suggested that one way of understanding the Spirit is to see the Spirit as the personal love which the Father has for the Son and the Son for the Father. In that understanding, we are invited to share in this inner and loving life of God, by having the Spirit live within us. Some of the most evocative names and descriptions of God in the New Testament are ways of drawing us in to this inner life. "The one who searches the hearts," writes Paul, "knows what the Spirit is thinking, because the Spirit intercedes for God's people according to God's will" (Romans 8:27). "The heart-searcher"—there's a divine name to ponder.

And it's all because of Jesus. Once we glimpse the doctrine—or the fact!—of the Trinity, we dare not slide back into a generalized sense of a religion paying distant homage to a god who (though somewhat more complicated than we had previously realized) is merely a quasi-personal source of general benevolence. Christian faith is much more hard-edged, more craggy, than that. Jesus exploded into the life of ancient Israel—the life of the whole world, in fact—not as a teacher of timeless truths, nor as a great moral example, but as the one through whose life, death, and resurrection God's rescue operation was put into effect, and the cosmos turned its great corner at last. All worldviews are challenged to the core by this claim. When they in turn challenge Christianity, it stands up remarkably well. It is because of Jesus that Christians claim they know who the creator God of the world really is. It is because he, a human being, is now with the Father in the dimension we call "heaven" that Christians came so quickly to speak of God as both Father and Son. It is because he remains as yet in heaven while we are on earth (though the Spirit makes him present to us) that Christians came to speak of the Spirit, too, as a distinct member of the divine Trinity. It is all because of Jesus that we speak of God the way we do.

And it is all because of Jesus that we find ourselves called to live the way we do. More particularly, it is through Jesus that we are summoned to become more truly human, to reflect the image of God into the world.

Part Three

Reflecting the Image

Eleven

Worship

When we begin to glimpse the reality of God, the natural reaction is to worship him. Not to have that reaction is a fairly sure sign that we haven't yet really understood who he is or what he's done.

So what is worship? The best way to discover is to join in and find out. However, many people who do that for a while, or even for their whole lives, find themselves getting stuck in the routine. They begin to ask deeper questions about what it all means, and why they do it. And many who don't join in with worship, or who used to but stopped a long time ago, remain puzzled as to the point of it all. For people in any of these categories, and indeed for people who enjoy worship but want to go deeper, a good place to start is the fourth and fifth chapters of the last book of the Bible, the Revelation of St. John.

Here we find ourselves eavesdropping on a majestic mystery. John the "seer," who is describing a vision he has seen, is himself something of a fly on the wall, peeping into the very throne room of God himself. We, watching the scene through his eyes, are eavesdropping at second hand, as it were. All the same, the scene tells us a great deal about worshipping the one true God.

John has been privileged to watch something going on in heaven. This doesn't mean that he has been fast-forwarded to some remote future. In fact, when he describes the ultimate future at the end of the book, it doesn't look like this earlier vision at all. Nor does it mean that he's been snatched off to some distant location far up in the sky. Rather, when he says that "a door stood open in heaven," he is insisting on one of the main points of this present book—namely, that God's sphere and ours are not far apart, and that at certain places and moments they interlock. Sometimes the boundary between them is like a thin partition, in which, to some people and at some times, a door is opened or a curtain pulled back, so that people in our dimension can see what's going on in God's dimension. What John sees in his vision is the regular life of heaven, the worship of God which, in that dimension, is going on all the time.

It is an astonishing sight. John begins by describing God's throne and even—though cautiously and obliquely—God himself. Thunder and lightning are coming from the throne, telling us that this is a place of majesty and awesome glory. Around the throne are representatives of the animal kingdom and the world of humanity: the whole creation is worshipping God for all he's worth. The animals are singing a song of God's eternal holiness:

Holy, holy, holy,
the Lord God the Almighty,
who was and is and is to come.

The animals and birds know their maker and praise him in a language humans wouldn't normally understand. But in the heavenly dimension all becomes clear. They know that their creator is all-powerful. They know that he is eternal. And they know that he is holy.

Already we see the inner logic of worship. Worship means, literally, acknowledging the *worth* of something or someone. It means recognizing and saying that something or someone is *worthy* of praise. It means celebrating the worth of someone or something far superior to oneself.

The scene that John depicts doesn't stop with a single song of praise; in fact, the scene is only just beginning. The animal creation praises God ceaselessly; the humans join in. But now their song is fuller, because they have something more to say; they cast their crowns before God's throne, not just to celebrate his greatness but also to express their *understanding* of why they, as his creatures, are right to offer him praise:

> You are worthy, our Lord and God,
> to receive glory and honor and power;
> for you created all things,
> and by your will they existed and were created.

Here we see God's world as it should be, God's world as it already is within the dimension of heaven. All creation worships God; human beings, through their chosen representatives, worship God because they have grasped an essential secret: they know why God *ought* to be praised, and why they *want* to praise him—because he has made all things.

This is the point at which most of us want to say, But the world is a mess! It's all very well for people to praise God as creator—but look at the state of his creation! What's he going to do about it?

The good news—and this is also right at the heart of what Christian worship is all about—is that exactly this reaction takes place before our eyes in the heavenly court itself. At the start of the fifth chapter of Revelation, John notices that the figure on the throne is holding a scroll, which we gradually realize is the scroll of God's future purposes, the purposes through which the world is at last to be judged and healed. The problem, however, is that nobody is able to open the scroll. God has committed himself, ever since creation, to working *through* his creatures—in particular, through his image-bearing human beings—but they have all let him down. For a moment it looks as though all God's plans are going to be thwarted.

But then there appears, beside the throne, a different kind of animal. He is, we are told, a Lion; but then we are also told that he is a Lamb. To read Revelation, you have to get used to its kaleidoscopic imagery. The Lion is an ancient Jewish image for the Messiah, the king of Israel and the world. The Lamb is the customary sacrificial offering for the sins of Israel and the world. Both these roles are combined in Jesus in a way that nobody had ever imagined before but that now makes perfect sense. And when he—the Lion/Lamb—appears, those who were already singing (the animals and the humans) turn their praise of God the creator into their praise of God the redeemer:

> You are worthy to take the scroll and to open its seals,
> for you were slaughtered and by your blood you ransomed for God
> saints from every tribe and language and people and nation;
> you have made them to be a kingdom and priests serving our God,
> and they will reign on earth.

Then, like a great oratorio with more choirs joining in from all directions, the angels take up the song:

> Worthy is the Lamb that was slaughtered
> to receive power and wealth and wisdom and might
> and honor and glory and blessing!

And, at last, "every creature in heaven and on earth and under the earth and in the sea, and all that is in them," join in the song:

> To the one seated on the throne and to the Lamb
> be blessing and honor and glory and might, forever and ever. Amen!

That is what worship is all about. It is the glad shout of praise that arises to God the creator and God the rescuer from the creation that recognizes its maker, the creation that acknowledges the triumph of Jesus the Lamb. That is the worship that is going on in heaven, in God's dimension, all the time. The question we ought to be asking is how best we might join in.

The Results of Worship

Because that is what we are supposed to do. And let's get one thing clear before we go any further. There is always a suspicion that creeps into discussions of this kind, a niggling worry that the call to worship God is rather like the order that goes out from a dictator whose subjects may not like him but have learned to fear him. He wants a hundred thousand people to line the route for his birthday parade? Very well, he shall have them, and they will all be cheering and waving as if their lives depended on it—because, in fact, they do. Turn away in boredom, or don't turn up at all, and it will be the worse for you.

If it has crossed your mind that worshipping the true God is like that, let me offer you a very different model. I have been to many concerts of music ranging from major symphonic works to big-band jazz. I have heard world-class orchestras under world-famous conductors. I have been in the audience for some great performances that have moved me and fed me and satisfied me richly. But only two or three times in my life have I been in an audience which, the moment the conductor's baton came down for the last time, leaped to its feet in electrified excitement, unable to contain its enthusiastic delight and wonder at what it had just experienced. (American readers might like to know that English audiences are very sparing with standing ovations.)

That sort of response is pretty close to genuine worship. Something like that, but more so, is the mood of Revelation 4 and 5. That is what, when we come to worship the living God, we are being invited to join in.

What happens when you're at a concert like that is that everyone present feels that they have grown in stature. Something has happened to them: they are aware of things in a new way; the whole world looks different. It's a bit like falling in love. In fact, it *is* a kind of falling in love. And when you fall in love, when you're ready to throw yourself at the feet of your beloved, what you desire, above all, is union.

This brings us to the first of two golden rules at the heart of spirituality. *You become like what you worship.* When you gaze in awe, admiration, and wonder at something or someone, you begin to take on something of the character of the object of your worship. Those who worship money become, eventually, human calculating machines. Those who worship sex become obsessed with their own attractiveness or prowess. Those who worship power become more and more ruthless.

So what happens when you worship the creator God whose plan to rescue the world and put it to rights has been accomplished by the Lamb who was slain? The answer comes in the second golden rule: because you were made in God's image, *worship makes you more truly human.* When you gaze in love and gratitude at the God in whose image you were made, you do indeed grow. You discover more of what it means to be fully alive.

Conversely, when you give that same total worship to anything or anyone else, you shrink as a human being. It doesn't, of course, feel like that at the time. When you worship part of the creation as though it were the Creator himself—in other words, when you worship an idol—you may well feel a brief "high." But, like a hallucinatory drug, that worship achieves its effect at a cost: when the effect is over, you are less of a human being than you were to begin with. That is the price of idolatry.

The opportunity, the invitation, the summons is there before us: to come and worship the true God, the creator, the redeemer, and to become more truly human by doing so. Worship is at the very center of all Christian living. One of the main reasons that theology (trying to think straight about who God is) matters is that we are called to love God with all our heart, mind, soul, and strength. It matters that we learn more about who God is so that we can praise him more appropriately. Perhaps one of the reasons why so much worship, in some churches at least, appears unattractive to so many people is that we have forgotten, or covered up, the truth about the one we are worshipping. But whenever we even glimpse the truth, we are drawn back. Like groupies sneaking off work to see a rock star who's in town for just an hour or so, like fans waiting all night for a glimpse of a football team returning in triumph—only much more so!—those who come to recognize the God we see in Jesus, the Lion who is also the Lamb, will long to come and worship him.

But how?

Celebrating God—Through Scripture

Because Christian worship is the celebratory praise and adoration of God the *creator,* one of its key tasks is to tell, in a thousand different ways, the story of creation and new creation. But if we try merely to celebrate creation the way it now is, concealing its flaws and horrors behind pious language, Christian worship can easily deteriorate and become trivial or sentimental. Wise Christian worship takes fully into account the fact that creation has gone horribly wrong, has been so corrupted and spoiled that a great fault line runs right down the middle of it—and down the middle of all of us, who, as image-bearing human beings, were meant to be taking care of it. That's why Christian worship is also the glad celebration of God's action in the past in Jesus the Messiah, and of the promise that what he accomplished in dying for our sins will be completed. In other words, as in Revelation 5, worship of God as *redeemer,* the lover and rescuer of the world, must always accompany and complete the worship of God as *creator.* This means, of course, telling the story of the rescue operation as well as of creation. Indeed, it means telling the story of salvation precisely *as* the story of the rescue and renewal of creation.

Telling the story, rehearsing the mighty acts of God: this is near the heart of Christian worship, a point not always fully appreciated in the enthusiastic, free-flowing worship common in many circles today. We know God through what he has done in creation, in Israel, and supremely in Jesus, and what he has done in his people and in the world through the Holy Spirit. Christian worship is praise of *this* God, the one who has done *these* things. And the place we find the God-given account of these events is of course scripture: the Bible.

I shall say more in due course about what the Bible itself is, but my point at the moment is simply this: reading the Bible aloud is always central to Christian worship. Cutting back on this for whatever reason—trimming readings so that the service doesn't go on too long, chanting scripture passages so that they become merely part of a musical performance, or reading only the few verses the preacher intends to preach about—misses the point. The reason we read scripture in worship isn't primarily to inform or remind the congregation about some biblical passage or theme they might have forgotten. Likewise, it's much more than a peg to hang a sermon on, though preaching from one or more of the readings is often a wise plan. Reading scripture in worship is, first and foremost, the central way of celebrating who God is and what he's done.

To be firmly practical for a moment: it is of course impossible, within the normal span of worship in most Western churches today, to read more than a chapter or two in the course of worship. But this ought not to blind us to what we are actually doing. Every time we meet for worship, every "service" we hold, is an occasion for celebrating the *whole* story of creation and salvation. We can't read the whole Bible in every service. But what we can and should do is to read two or more passages, preferably including at least one from the Old Testament.

Let me put it like this. The room I am sitting in at the moment has quite small windows. If I stand at the other side of the room, I can see only a little of what is outside—part of the house opposite, and a tiny bit of sky. But if I go up close to the window, I can see trees, fields, animals, the sea, the hills in the distance.

It sometimes feels as though two or three short biblical readings are rather like the windows seen from the other side of the room. We can't see very much through them. But as we get to know the Bible better, we get closer to the windows (as it were), so that, without the windows having gotten any bigger, we can glimpse the entire sweep of the biblical countryside.

Even the simplest acts of Christian worship ought therefore always to focus on the reading of scripture. Sometimes there will be a time for the congregation to meditate on one or more of the readings. Sometimes there will be an opportunity to respond. The church has developed rich resources of material, taken not least from the Bible itself, which worshippers may sing or say by way of pondering what they've heard and continuing to thank God for it.

That's how Christian worship begins to develop a particular shape, a "liturgy": as a showcase for scripture, a way of making sure that the faithful are treating it with the seriousness it deserves. Just as you're insulting a good wine if you drink it from a plastic cup instead of a glass which shows off its color, bouquet, and full flavor, so you're insulting the Bible if, given the opportunity, you don't create a context in which it can be heard and celebrated as what it really is: the rehearsal of the powerful deeds of God the creator and rescuer.

Of course, if you're thirsty and a plastic cup is all you have, go ahead. There are times when (for a picnic, say) you might actually choose plastic over glass. Better to worship God even chaotically than not at all. But for normal purposes, we choose a glass to match the wine.

In particular, Christian worship from very earliest times has made good use of the Psalms. They are inexhaustible, and deserve to be read, said, sung, chanted, whispered, learned by heart, and even shouted from the rooftops. They express all the emotions we are ever likely to feel (including some we hope we may not), and they lay them, raw and open, in the presence of God, like a golden retriever bringing to its master's feet every strange object it finds in the field. "Look!" says the Psalmist. "This is what I've found today! Isn't that extraordinary? What are you going to do with it?"

The Psalms join together what often look to us like polar opposites as we come into God's presence. They pass swiftly from loving intimacy to thunderstruck awe and back again. They bring together sharp, angry questioning and simple, quiet trust. They range from the gentle and meditative to the loud and boisterous, from lament and black despair to solemn and holy celebration. There's a wonderful peace that comes in working through from the great cry that opens Psalm 22 ("My God, my God, why have you forsaken me?") to its concluding confident assertion that God has heard and answered the prayer, and then stepping straight into the serene trust and assurance of Psalm 23 ("The Lord is my Shepherd"). There's a wise and healthy balance about reading, one after the other, the resounding triumphalism of Psalm 136 ("He struck down great kings, for his steadfast loves endures forever; and killed famous kings, for his steadfast loves endures forever," with the cheerful little refrain bouncing along in every line throughout the whole Psalm) and the shattering desolation of Psalm 137 ("By the waters of Babylon we sat down and wept").

Of course we will never understand everything in the Psalms. Of course there will be puzzles and problems. Some churches, some congregations, and some Christians will find that this ancient poetry contains passages they can't use in good conscience—particularly those lines that call down bitter curses on their enemies. That's a decision that must be made in each local church. But no Christian congregation ought to deny itself regular and thorough use of the Psalms. One of the great tragedies in much contemporary free-church worship is the great void at this point. Here is a challenge for a new generation of musicians to take up. And here, too, is a challenge for those traditions, like my own, in which the Psalms have always been front and center: Are we making the best use of them? Are we going deeper and deeper into them, or simply round and round in circles?

The Bible is, in short, the staple diet of Christian worship, as it is of Christian teaching. But, as one of the most famous stories in scripture makes abundantly clear, even scripture isn't the very center. When the risen Jesus met two disciples on the road to Emmaus, their hearts burned within them while he talked about the Bible. But their eyes were opened, and they recognized him, when he broke the bread.

Celebrating God—Through the Breaking of Bread

Lord's Supper, Holy Communion, Eucharist, Mass—it almost sounds like a child's rhyme ("tinker, tailor, soldier, sailor"). And the first thing to be said is: *the name doesn't matter.* No, really it doesn't. There was a time when huge theological, cultural, and political battles hung on how you interpreted what was said and done at the bread-breaking service (to give it a neutral name), and which label you put on it. That time has virtually disappeared. Without everyone realizing it, there has been considerable convergence among most Christian churches over the last few decades as to what they think is happening at this central service, what it means, and how we can best profit from it. There are still, of course, residual problems. I hope this part of the chapter will begin to dispel some of them.

Three opening remarks. First, we break bread and drink wine together, telling the story of Jesus and his death, because Jesus knew that this set of actions would explain the meaning of his death in a way that nothing else—no theories, no clever ideas—could ever do. After all, when Jesus died for our sins it wasn't so he could fill our minds with true ideas, however important they may be, but so he could *do* something, namely, rescue us from evil and death.

Second, it isn't a piece of sympathetic magic, as suspicious Protestants have often worried it might be. This action, like the symbolic actions performed by the ancient prophets, becomes one of the points at which heaven and earth coincide. Paul says that "as often as you eat the bread and drink the cup, you *proclaim* the Lord's death until he comes" (1 Corinthians 11:26). He doesn't mean that it's a good opportunity for a sermon. Like a handshake or a kiss, *doing* it *says* it.

Third, therefore, nor is the bread-breaking a mere occasion for remembering something that happened a long time ago, as suspicious Catholics sometimes suppose Protestants believe. When we break the bread and drink the wine, we find ourselves joining the disciples in the Upper Room. We are united with Jesus himself as he prays in Gethsemane and stands before Caiaphas and Pilate. We become one with him as he hangs on the cross and rises from the tomb. Past and present come together. Events from long ago are fused with the meal we are sharing here and now.

But it isn't only the past that comes forward into the present. If the bread-breaking is one of the key moments when the thin partition between heaven and earth becomes transparent, it is also one of the key moments when God's future comes rushing into the present. Like the children of Israel still in the wilderness, tasting food which the spies had brought back from their secret trip to the Promised Land, in the bread-breaking we are tasting God's new creation—the new creation whose prototype and origin is Jesus himself.

That is one of the reasons why he said "This is my body" and "This is my blood." We don't need elaborate metaphysical theories with long Latin names to get the point. Jesus—the real Jesus, the living Jesus, the Jesus who dwells in heaven and rules over earth as well, the Jesus who has brought God's future into the present—wants not just to influence us, but to rescue us; not just to inform us, but to heal us; not just to give us something to think about, but to feed us, and to feed us with himself. That's what this meal is all about.

Perhaps the biggest problem that Christians in Protestant churches have faced about this meal is the idea that it is a "good

work," which people "do" in order to earn God's favor. Some Protestants still feel that way about *anything* that is "done" in church;
though unless we are to sit absolutely still and say nothing at all, we
are bound to "do" *something* in our worship together. Even choosing to be silent, as in a Quaker meeting, is a choice to do something—namely, to come together and be silent. Of course, there is
a danger that fussy ritual will forget what it's there for and become
an end in itself. Think back to the wineglass and the plastic cup:
there are some churches where (so to speak) the wineglasses are
the best that money can buy, but nobody bothers anymore about
the quality of the wine. Equally, there are some that are so proud
of having gotten rid of the fancy wineglasses and gone in for plastic cups that they, too, are concentrating on the outward form rather than the real meaning.

That danger, you see, is not confined to "high-church" ritual.
It is not only present when people insist on crossing themselves at
exactly the right moment and in exactly the right manner; it is just
as present when people insist on raising their arms in the air during worship, or indeed when they insist on *not* crossing themselves,
raising their arms, or doing any other action. I have on occasion
been wryly amused when a church has abandoned its robed choir
and organist because they seemed too "professional," and have then
employed half a dozen people to spend the whole service twiddling knobs and pushing sliders to control the sound, the lights,
and the overhead projector. *Anything* that needs to be done during
worship can become a ritual performed for its own sake. Likewise,
anything that needs to be done during worship can be done as an
act of pure gratitude, a glad response to free grace.

Having said that, we can now see what might be meant by
speaking, as some Christian traditions have done, of the bread-
breaking service as a "sacrifice." This has been controversial for a
long time, and two mistakes have often been made in the debate.
First, people sometimes supposed that the point of a sacrifice, in the
Old Testament, was for the worshipper to "do" something to earn

God's favor. Not so. That rests on a misunderstanding of the Jewish Law itself, in which the sacrifices were required by God, and were offered in thanksgiving, not as an attempt to bribe or placate God but as a way of responding to his love. We can't, of course, know what was in the hearts of all ancient Jews as they worshipped. But the system certainly wasn't designed as a way of twisting God's arm, but as a way of responding to his love.

Second, there has been endless confusion over the relationship between the bread-breaking service and the sacrifice offered by Jesus on the cross. Catholics have usually said that they were one and the same, to which Protestants have replied that the Catholic interpretation looks like an attempt to repeat something which was done once and once only, and can never be done again. Protestants have usually said that the bread-breaking service is a *different* sacrifice to the one offered by Jesus—they see it as a "sacrifice of praise" offered by the worshippers—to which Catholics have responded that the Protestant interpretation looks like an attempt to add something to the already complete offering of Jesus, which (they say) becomes "sacramentally" present in the bread and the wine.

I believe that we can move beyond these sterile disputes by putting our discussion of worship within our larger picture of heaven and earth, of God's future and our present, and of the way in which those two pairs come together in Jesus and the Spirit. Within the biblical worldview (which has not so much been disproved as ignored in much modern thought), heaven and earth overlap, and do so at certain specific times and places, Jesus and the Spirit being the key markers. In the same way, at certain places and moments God's future and God's past (that is, events like Jesus's death and resurrection) arrive in the present—rather as though you were to sit down to a meal and discover your great-great-grandparents, and also your great-great-grandchildren, turning up to join you. That's how God's time works. That's why Christian worship is what it is.

This, I believe, sets the right framework for all our thinking about worship, and all discussion of the church's sacramental life. The rest is footnotes, temperament, tradition, and—let's face it—individual likes and dislikes (which is what I call them when they're mine) and irrational prejudices (which is what I call them when they're yours). And at that point the two great commands in the Law (loving God, loving our neighbor) ought to remind us what to do. As Christians we should expect to have demands made on our charity and our patience. Let's not keep robbing ourselves and our churches of the full enjoyment of the central act of Christian worship by making this meal an occasion of strife.

Worshipping Together

I've spoken throughout this chapter about the corporate, public worship of the church. From the beginning it was clear that Christianity is something people do *together*. Having said that, the earliest writers were also concerned that all members of the Body of Christ should be awake and active in personal faith; should know their own responsibilities and make real for themselves the privilege of worship. That way, when the whole assembly gathers together, each will have his or her own joy and sorrow, insight and question, to bring.

For that reason it is right and proper that every Christian, and if possible every Christian household, should learn the habits of worship alone and in small groups. Similar principles apply, with (no doubt) endless local variations. What matters is not so much *how* we go about it as *that* we go about it. Think back to Revelation 4 and 5. The whole creation is worshipping God. We are invited not only to watch, like flies on the wall, but to join in the song. How can you refuse?

Twelve

Prayer

Our Father in heaven
Hallowed be your name.
Your kingdom come,
Your will be done, on earth as it is in heaven.
Give us this day our daily bread.
Forgive us our debts, as we too have forgiven our debtors.
Do not bring us to the time of trial,
But rescue us from the evil one.
For the kingdom, the power, and the glory are yours,
Now and forever. Amen.

All right, I know: everyone prefers a slightly different translation. I love the traditional one I grew up with, but I have become used to other ones as well. There are problems deciding what the "real" wording is, not least because the Greek versions of the prayer (in Matthew, Luke, and a very early Christian book called "The Teaching") aren't quite the same, haven't always got exact word-by-word English equivalents, and may not reproduce exactly the flavor of the Aramaic prayer Jesus himself probably used. But again, *the precise wording doesn't matter.* Don't allow the surface noise to put you off.

Go instead for the heart of it. It's a prayer about God's honor and glory. It's a prayer about God's kingdom coming on earth as in heaven—which, as we've seen, pretty much sums up what a lot of Christianity is all about. It's a prayer for bread, for meeting the needs of every day. And it's a prayer for rescue from evil.

At every point, the prayer reflects what Jesus himself was doing in his work. It isn't a general prayer to a generalized "divinity" or "godhead." It isn't even a typical Jewish prayer (though almost every element in it can be matched to Jewish prayers of the period). The prayer is, so to speak, Jesus-specific.

It was, after all, Jesus who was going around saying it was time for the Father's name to be honored, for his kingdom to come on earth as in heaven. It was Jesus who fed the crowds with bread in the desert. It was Jesus who forgave sinners and told his followers to do the same. It was Jesus who walked, clear-eyed, into the "time of trial," the great tribulation that was rushing like a tidal wave upon Israel and the world, so that by taking its full force on himself others might be spared it. And it was Jesus who was inaugurating God's kingdom, exercising God's power, and dying and rising to display God's glory. The "Lord's Prayer," as we call it, grows directly out of what Jesus was doing in Galilee. And Gethsemane, too: the prayer looks directly forward to what he achieved in his death and resurrection.

The prayer is therefore a way of saying to the Father: Jesus has (in the image he himself used) caught me in the net of his good news. The prayer says: I want to be part of his kingdom-movement. I find myself drawn into his heaven-on-earth way of living. I want to be part of his bread-for-the-world agenda, for myself and for others. I need forgiveness for myself—from sin, from debt, from every weight around my neck—and I intend to live with forgiveness in my heart in my own dealings with others. (Notice how remarkable it is that, at the heart of the prayer, we commit ourselves to live in a particular way, a way we find difficult.) And because I live in the real world, where evil is still powerful, I need protecting and rescuing. And, in and through it all, I acknowledge and celebrate the Father's kingdom, power, and glory.

Most of the things we might want to pray about are taken care of within that prayer. Like Jesus's parables, it is small in scale but huge in coverage. Some people find that it helps to pray the Lord's Prayer slowly, pausing every few words to hold before God the particular things on their hearts which come into that category. Some people prefer to use it at the beginning or the end of a more extended time of prayer, either to set the context for everything else or to sum things up. Some people find that saying it slowly, over and over again, helps them to go down deeply into the love and presence of God, into the place where the spheres overlap, into the power of the gospel to bring bread and forgiveness and rescue. However you want to use it, use it. Start here and see where it takes you.

Prayer Between Heaven and Earth

Christian prayer is simple, in the sense that a small child can pray the prayer Jesus taught. But it's hard in the demands it makes as we go on with it. The agony of the Psalmist reached its own climax when Jesus wept and sweated blood in Gethsemane, struggling with his Father about the final step in his lifelong vocation. That led, in turn, to his hanging in despair on the cross, with the first verse of Psalm 22 ("My God, why did you abandon me?") all that was left to say, the God-given way of shouting out his Godforsakenness. When Jesus told us to take up our cross and follow him, he presumably expected that following him would include moments like that for us, too.

We are called to live at the overlap both of heaven and earth—the earth that has yet to be fully redeemed as one day it will be—and of God's future and this world's present. We are caught on a small island near the point where these tectonic plates—heaven and earth, future and present—are scrunching themselves together. Be ready for earthquakes! When Paul writes his greatest chapter about life in the Spirit and the coming renewal of the whole cosmos, he points out at the heart of it all that, while we don't know how to pray as we ought, the Spirit—God's very own Spirit—intercedes for us according to God's will. It's a small passage (Romans 8:26–27), but it's extremely important both for what it says and for where it says it. Here's the context: God's whole creation is groaning in labor pains, says Paul, waiting for the new world to be born from its womb. The church, God's people in the Messiah, find themselves caught up in this, as we, too, groan in longing for redemption. (Paul was talking, a few verses earlier, about sharing the sufferings of the Messiah. Did he, perhaps, have Gethsemane in mind?) Christian prayer is at its most characteristic when we find ourselves caught in the overlap of the ages, part of the creation that aches for new birth.

And the strange new promise, the point at which Christian prayer is marked out over against pantheism and Deism and a good deal else besides, is that, by the Spirit, *God himself is groaning from within the heart of the world, because God himself, by the Spirit, dwells in our hearts as we resonate with the pain of the world.* This isn't the pantheistic getting-in-touch-with-the-heart-of-things. This is the strange, new getting-in-touch-with-the-living-God, who is doing a new thing, who has come to the heart of the world in Jesus precisely because all is not well (a point the pantheist can never acknowledge) and it needs to be put right, who now comes by his Spirit to the place where the world is in pain (a point the Deist can never contemplate) in order that, *in and through us—those who pray in Christ and by the Spirit—*the groaning of all creation may come before the Father himself, the heart-searcher (8:27), the one who works all things together for good for those who love him (8:28). This is what it means to be "conformed to the image of his Son" (8:29). This is what it means, within the present age, to share his glory (8:18, 30).

This explains why specifically Christian prayer makes the sense it does within the world where heaven and earth belong together. It is worth developing the picture we sketched earlier, to show how prayer within the Christian worldview is significantly different from prayer as seen from within the two other main options.

For the pantheist, living in Option One, prayer is simply getting in tune with the deepest realities of the world and of oneself. Divinity is everywhere, including within me. Prayer is therefore not so much addressing someone else, who lives somewhere else, but rather discovering and getting in tune with an inner truth and life that are to be found deep within my own heart and within the silent rhythms of the world around. That is pantheistic prayer. It is (in my judgment) a lot healthier than pagan prayer, where a human being tries to invoke, placate, cajole, or bribe the sea-god, the war-god, the river-god, or the marriage-god to get special favors or avoid particular dangers. Compared with that, pantheistic prayer has a certain stately nobility about it. But it isn't Christian prayer.

For the Deist, living in Option Two, prayer is calling across a void to a distant deity. This lofty figure may or may not be listening. He, or it, may or may not be inclined, or even able, to do very much about us and our world, even if he (or it) wanted to. So, at the extreme of Option Two, all you can do is send off a message, like a marooned sailor scribbling a note and putting it in a bottle, on the off-chance that someone out there might pick it up. That kind of prayer takes a good deal of faith and hope. But it isn't Christian prayer.

Sometimes, of course, prayer within the Jewish and Christian traditions feels exactly like the prayer of Option Two, as the Psalms themselves bear witness. But, for the Psalmist, the sense of a void, an emptiness where there ought to be a Presence, isn't something to accept calmly as the way things simply are. It is something to complain at, to jump up and down about. "Wake up, YHWH!" shouts the Psalmist, like someone standing at the foot of the bed, hands on hips, looking crossly at a sleeping form. (That is of course how the disciples addressed Jesus, asleep in the boat during the storm.) "It's time to get up and *do* something about this mess!"

But the whole point of the Christian story, at the climax of the Jewish story, is that the curtain has been pulled back, the door has been opened from the other side, and like Jacob we have glimpsed a ladder between heaven and earth with messengers going to and fro upon it. "The kingdom of heaven is at hand," says Jesus in Matthew's gospel, not offering a new way of getting to heaven hereafter, but announcing that the rule of heaven, the very *life* of heaven, is now overlapping with earth in a new way—a way which sweeps together all the moments from Jacob's ladder to Isaiah's vision, all the patriarchal insights and prophetic dreams, and turns them into a human form, a human voice, a human life, a human death. Jesus is the reason for Option Three; and, with that, prayer has come of age. Heaven and earth have overlapped permanently where he stands, where he hung, where he rises, wherever the fresh wind of his Spirit now blows. Living as a Christian means living in the world as it's been reshaped by and around Jesus and his Spirit. And that means that Christian prayer is a different kind of thing—different both from the prayer of the pantheist, getting in touch with the inwardness of nature, and that of the Deist, sending out messages across a lonely emptiness.

Christian prayer is about standing at the fault line, being shaped by the Jesus who knelt in Gethsemane, groaning in travail, holding heaven and earth together like someone trying to tie two pieces of rope with people tugging at the other ends to pull them apart. It goes, quite closely, with the triple identity of the true God at which we stared, dazzled, in the previous section of this book. No wonder we give up so easily. No wonder we need help.

Fortunately, there is plenty available.

Discovering Help in Prayer

Help is at hand not least in those who have trodden the path ahead of us. Part of our difficulty here is that we moderns are so anxious to do things our own way, so concerned that if we get help from anyone else our prayer won't be "authentic" and come from our own heart, that we are instantly suspicious about using anyone else's prayers. We are like someone who doesn't feel she's properly dressed unless she has personally designed and made all her own clothes; or like someone who feels it's artificial to drive a car he hasn't built all by himself. We are hamstrung by the long legacy of the Romantic movement on the one hand, and Existentialism on the other, producing the idea that things are authentic only if they come spontaneously, unbidden, from the depths of our hearts.

Frankly, as Jesus pointed out, there's a lot that comes from the depths of our hearts which may be authentic but isn't very pretty. One good breath of fresh air from the down-to-earth world of first-century Judaism is enough to blow away the smog of the self-absorbed (and ultimately proud) quest for "authenticity" of that kind. When Jesus's followers asked him to teach them to pray, he didn't tell them to divide into focus groups and look deep within their own hearts. He didn't begin by getting them to think slowly through their life experiences to discover what types of personality each of them had, to spend time getting in touch with their buried feelings. He and they both understood the question they had asked: they wanted, and needed, *a form of words which they could learn and use.* That's what John the Baptist had given to his followers. Other Jewish teachers had done the same. That's what Jesus did, too, giving his disciples the prayer we began with at the start of this chapter, which remains at the heart of all Christian prayer.

But notice the point. There's nothing wrong with having a form of words composed by somebody else. Indeed, there's probably something wrong with *not* using such a form. Some Christians, some of the time, can sustain a life of prayer entirely out of their own internal resources, just as there are hardy mountaineers (I've met one) who can walk the Scottish highlands in their bare feet. But most of us need boots; not because we don't want to do the walking ourselves, but because we do.

This plea, it will be obvious, is aimed in one particular direction: at the growing number of Christians in many countries who, without realizing it, are absorbing an element of late modern culture (the Romantic-plus-Existentialist mixture I mentioned a moment ago) as though it were Christianity itself. To them I want to say: there is nothing wrong, nothing sub-Christian, nothing to do with "works-righteousness," about using words, set forms, prayers, and sequences of prayers written by other people in other centuries. Indeed, the idea that I must always find my own words, that I must generate my own devotion from scratch every morning, that unless I think of new words I must be spiritually lazy or deficient—that has the all-too-familiar sign of human pride, of "doing it my way": of, yes, works-righteousness. Good liturgy—other people's prayers, whether for corporate or individual use—can be, *should* be, a sign and means of grace, an occasion of humility (accepting that someone else has said, better than I can, what I deeply want to express) and gratitude. How many times have I been grateful, faced with nightfalls both metaphorical and literal, for the old Anglican prayer which runs,

Lighten our darkness, we beseech thee, O Lord;
and by thy great mercy
defend us from all perils and dangers of this night;
for the love of thy only Son,
our Savior Jesus Christ. Amen.

I didn't write it, but whoever did has my undying gratitude. It's just what I wanted.

Of course, there's a plea to be directed the other way as well. The Romantics and the Existentialists were not fools. Some suits of clothes don't fit; they constrict both movement and personality. Some walking boots are too cumbersome. When David went off to fight Goliath, he couldn't wear the heavy armor which tradition suggested. He had to use the simpler weapons he already knew. They worked for him. If it weren't so tragic, it would be hugely comic to watch many people in traditional churches clumping around in suits of armor made for serious warfare—in other words, using ancient liturgies and traditional practices—without much apparent idea where they're going or what to do when they get there. Old forms and traditions of worship and prayer can indeed be a way of fueling genuine prayer, of enabling people to come with humility into the presence of God and to discover that, bit by bit, prayers that have served other generations well can become their own heartfelt outpourings, too. But living traditions can turn quite quickly into deadweight. Sometimes last year's deadwood needs to be cleared away to make room for new growth.

David, remember, handpicked five stones that had been worn smooth by a brook. There are many prayers which, worn smooth by many generations, are now at hand and ready for use. But David, precisely because of his victory over Goliath, became king, and had to work out the quite different skills needed to run a court and a country. As our culture changes, and as change itself becomes the most constant feature of our culture, we shouldn't be surprised that many people find traditional forms puzzling and off-putting. I've met people in the last year or two who have stopped going to their local church because people have started singing new songs and dancing in the aisles. And I've met others who have *started* going for precisely the same reason. It's time to give ourselves a shake—to recognize that different people need different kinds of help at different stages of their lives—and get on with it.

But for a great many Christians, discovering that there are ways of being helped in prayer by using words and forms written and shaped by others comes as good news, as a sigh of relief. Prayers like the one I quoted a moment ago are there to help us grow, not to keep us shrunken. And there is much, much more: books of prayers, anthologies of meditations, shelves and libraries full of material, something for everyone. And if that all seems too daunting, remember the advice of a wise parent to the child who panicked after undertaking a massive school project on ornithology. Just take it bird by bird.

More Pathways into Prayer

The Lord's Prayer isn't the only prayer that has formed the basis of deep and rich traditions of Christian praying. There are other prayers which have been used in similar ways through the years, either as a pattern or as something to repeat in order to go down deeper into the presence of the God we know in Jesus. Perhaps the best known of these, widely practiced in the Eastern Orthodox churches, is the "Jesus Prayer," which can be said easily and slowly with the rhythm of one's breathing: "Lord Jesus Christ, Son of the Living God, have mercy on me, a sinner."

Much has been written about this prayer—what it means, how to use it, where it can take you. It isn't as restrictive as it seems at first sight. Praying for mercy doesn't just mean "I've done something wrong, so please forgive me." It's a much wider petition, asking that God send his merciful presence and help in a thousand and one situations, despite the fact that we don't deserve such aid and never could. And, though the prayer is explicitly addressed to Jesus himself, which is unusual though not unknown even in the New Testament itself, it's offered in the confidence that when we come to Jesus we thereby come through him to the Father; and that, in order to pray that way, we need to be led by the Holy Spirit.

Saying this prayer (or others like it) over and over again isn't, then, the kind of "heaping up of empty phrases" which Jesus criticizes as a typically pagan practice in Matthew 6:7. Of course, if it becomes that kind of thing for you, drop it and do something different. But for millions of people it has been, and still is, a way of coming into focus, of going down deep and out wide, of concentrating on the God we know in Jesus as the one we can trust in all circumstances, and of holding before his mercy all that we want to pray about—delights, problems, sorrows, angers, fears, other people, government policies, social problems, wars, disasters, celebrations.

I have sometimes suggested two other similar prayers to go alongside the Jesus Prayer: "Father Almighty, maker of heaven and earth, set up your kingdom in our midst"; and "Holy Spirit, breath of the living God, renew me and all the world." These can be said in the same way; or they, and the Jesus Prayer itself, can be used as recurring phrases to enable a group or congregation to join together while prayers are said for particular people and situations. Whether a person is praying alone or with others, there's plenty of room to experiment here, as elsewhere.

There's one more prayer I'd like to mention which can be used like this, and which I suspect was used like this in the very earliest church. From ancient to modern Judaism, one prayer has been said three times a day. It begins, "Hear, O Israel; YHWH our God, YHWH is one; and you shall love YHWH your God with all your heart." This opening sentence is found in Deuteronomy 6:4; it's known as the *Shema* Prayer, because the opening word, "Hear," is *Shema* in Hebrew. People are sometimes surprised to hear this verse referred to as a *prayer,* since it looks more like a theological statement with a command attached; but, just as reading scripture in worship is done not to tell the congregation something they didn't know, but to praise God for what he's done, in the same way declaring who YHWH truly is, and what he requires of his covenant people, is indeed a prayer, an act of worship and commitment. It is a means precisely of turning away from oneself and one's own list of needs, wants, hopes, and fears and placing all one's attention on God, God's name, God's nature, God's intentions, God's invitation to love him, God's glory. Even thinking through the fact that this prayer *is* a prayer is thus highly instructive.

But in very early Christianity this Jewish prayer grew—because of Jesus. As we saw in Chapter Ten, Paul reminded the Corinthian Christians that they were Jewish-style monotheists, not pagan polytheists; and, to make the point, he quoted this prayer in its new, Christian form (1 Corinthians 8:6). For us, he says,

> There is one God, the Father,
> from whom are all things, and we to him;

and one Lord, Jesus the Messiah,
through whom are all things, and we through him.

Having spoken just before about our love for God, Paul then goes on, in the passage immediately following, to speak of our love for one another, the love which flows precisely from the fact that we believe the Messiah died for our neighbor as well as for ourselves.

Why should we not make this prayer, too, our own? Like the Jesus Prayer, it can be said slowly and repeatedly. Like the great hymns of praise in Revelation 4 and 5, it sums up the worship and praise of God as both creator and redeemer. (The shorthand "from whom . . . to him" and "through whom . . . through him" are dense but clear statements of the Father as the source and goal of all things, and of the Son as the means by whom all things were made and all things redeemed. (Paul says the same thing more fully in Colossians 1:15–20.) To meditate on God in this way is to gaze out, like a balloonist on a clear day, over the whole majestic landscape of the loving purposes of God, enabling us to pick out this or that particular feature for special attention without losing the larger sweep of the whole. The early Christians clearly knew a thing or two about prayer. We can still learn a great deal from them.

Getting Started

There is (of course) much more that could be said about prayer, but, as with worship, the important thing is to get on with it. There are many guides available. One of the signs of health in contemporary Christianity is that more and more people recognize that talking to an experienced guide (known in some traditions as a "spiritual director") can be a great help—both a reassurance ("Yes, it's all right; a lot of people feel like that") and a gentle prompter in new directions. I well remember the sense of relief I felt when my spiritual director suggested that, faced with a particularly dif-

ficult colleague, I should try saying the Lord's Prayer and thinking of each petition as applying to him in particular. Books, retreat
leaders, friends, and local clergy can all help. Although Jesus took a
brisk approach to the request, "Teach us to pray," it's of course true
that different people will find different patterns and pathways helpful, and there are plenty of teachers who can point out the way forward for particular people and particular situations.

Likewise, anyone can get a notebook and organize into daily or
weekly lists the people and situations they want to pray for. Even
those who can't bear lists at any price may find that a diary and
an address book, and perhaps even a map, will remind them of situations and people. There will be things to thank God for (gratitude is always a sign of grace) and things to say sorry for (penitence,
likewise). There will be things to ask for, not least in relation to
God's love and power surrounding and helping particular people
for whom we wish to pray. As we reach for some of the astonishing
promises in the New Testament ("If you abide in me," said Jesus,
"and my words abide in you, ask whatever you will, and it shall be
done" [John 15:7]), we discover that they are balanced by a strange
phenomenon. When we come eagerly to claim such promises, we
find that, if we are serious, our desires and hopes are gently but
firmly reshaped, sorted out, and put in fresh order.

There are plenty of other modes of Christian prayer. For some,
praying in tongues is a way of lifting things and people up to God
when we don't know what their particular needs are, or perhaps
when the need is all too blindingly obvious and we are so overwhelmed with it that we don't know what to say. (Back, once
more, to Romans 8:26–27.) For some, silence—difficult to attain
for many, difficult to maintain for most—can, like the best sort of
darkness, become the soil in which seeds of faith, hope, and love
can germinate unseen. But for all of us, Christian prayer is God's
gift. "Through the Messiah we have access, by faith, to this grace in
which we stand" (Romans 5:2). We are welcomed into God's very
presence. Like John in Revelation 4 and 5, we see through prayer a

door standing open in heaven, and we are ushered into the throne room.

But we are no longer there as mere observers. We are there as beloved children. Let Jesus himself have the last word: "If you, then, evil as you are, know how to give good gifts to your children, how much more will your Father in heaven give good things to those who ask him!" (Matthew 7:11).

Thirteen

✝

The Book God Breathed

It's a big book, full of big stories with big characters. They have big ideas (not least about themselves) and make big mistakes. It's about God and greed and grace; about life, lust, laughter, and loneliness. It's about birth, beginnings, and betrayal; about siblings, squabbles, and sex; about power and prayer and prison and passion.

And that's only Genesis.

The Bible itself, with Genesis as its majestic overture, is a huge, sprawling book. I've mentioned it often enough already, but now at last it's time to focus on what it is in itself. Imagine it as an enormous mural: if you painted all the figures life-size, you'd need most of the Great Wall of China to display it. Picking it up, you need to remind yourself that you hold in your hands not only the most famous book in the world, but one which has extraordinary power to change lives, to change communities, to change the world. It's done it before. It can do it again.

But surely (someone will say) only God gets to change the world like that? How can we say that a mere *book* can do such a thing?

That's the strange thing. That's why the Bible is nonnegotiable. It's a vital, central element in Christian faith and life. You can't do without it, even though too many Christians have forgotten what to do *with* it. Somehow, God seems to have delegated (as it were) some at least of the things he intends to do in the world to this book.

This process isn't quite like someone making a will, but nearly. It isn't quite like a composer writing a score for people to play, but it's not far off. It isn't exactly like a dramatist writing a play, but that gets quite close. It isn't even, though this is perhaps the sharpest yet, that the Bible is "the story so far" in the true novel that God is still writing. It's all of these and more.

That, no doubt, is why there are so many fights about it. In fact, there are just as many battles *about* the Bible these days as there are battles within its pages. And some of them are for the same reason. Sibling rivalry: from Cain and Abel to the two unnamed brothers in Jesus's story about the prodigal son, and now to the many varieties of Christianity in the world, each with its own way of reading the Bible. Each finds itself nourished and sustained by that reading. Each, supposedly, attempts to put into practice the lessons it learns.

Does it matter?

Well, yes, it does. Tragically, the history of Christianity is littered with ways of reading the Bible which have, in effect, muzzled it. The computer I'm writing on right now will do a thousand things, but I use it only for writing and for access to the Internet and email. In the same way, many Christians—whole generations of them, sometimes entire denominations—have in their possession a book which will do a thousand things not only in and for them but *through* them in the world. And they use it only to sustain the three or four things they already do. They treat it as a form of verbal wallpaper: pleasant enough in the background, but you stop thinking about it once you've lived in the house a few weeks. It really doesn't matter that I don't exploit more than a small amount of my computer's capability. But to be a Christian while not letting the Bible do all the things it's capable of, through you and in you, is like trying to play the piano with your fingers tied together.

So what is the Bible, and what should we be doing with it?

What Is the Bible?

To begin with, the facts. Those who know all this already might like to skip this section; but many who aren't familiar with scripture might want to be put in the picture.

The Bible consists of two parts, which Christians refer to as the "Old Testament" and the "New Testament." The Old Testament is much longer—nearly a thousand pages in the average printing, against the New Testament's three hundred. The Old Testament came into existence over a period of more than a millennium; the New, within less than a century.

The word "testament" is a translation of the word which also means "covenant." It's a central Christian claim that the events concerning Jesus were the means by which, in fulfillment of ancient Israelite prophecy, the creator God, Israel's God, renewed the covenant with Israel and thereby rescued the world. Many of the early Christian writings make the point by explicitly hooking on to the Old Testament, quoting or echoing it in order to offer themselves as the charter of that covenant renewal—hence, "New Testament." Calling the two parts by these related but differentiated names is thus a way of highlighting a claim and a question: the claim that the Jewish Bible remains a vital part of Christian scripture, and the question of how it is to be understood and applied by those who believe that its "covenant" was indeed renewed in Jesus.

The books which Jews call the Bible and Christians call the Old Testament were grouped in three sections. The first five books (Genesis, Exodus, Leviticus, Numbers, and Deuteronomy) were always regarded as foundational and special. They are known as the "Torah" ("Law"), and are traditionally ascribed to Moses himself. The next collection, known as the "Prophets," includes what we often think of as some of the historical books (1 and 2 Samuel, 1 and 2 Kings) as well as the books of the great prophets (Isaiah, Jeremiah, Ezekiel) and the so-called "minor" prophets (Hosea and the rest). The third division, headed by the Psalms, is known

simply as the "Writings," and includes some very ancient material and some parts—such as the book of Daniel—which were edited and accepted only within the last two hundred years BC. Even
around the time of Jesus some people were still debating whether all the Writings really belonged (Esther and the Song of Solomon being particularly contentious). Most thought they did, and
so it has remained.

Torah, Prophets, and Writings: thirty-nine books in all. It may
well be that the Law and the Prophets became fixed collections
considerably earlier than the Writings. One way or another, the
three sections became the official list of the sacred books of the
Jewish people. The Greek word for such an official list is "canon,"
which means "rule" or "measuring stick." That word, which we
encountered in our earlier discussion of the gospels, has been
applied to the Old Testament books since the third or fourth century of the Christian era.

Most of these books were written in Hebrew, which is why the
Old Testament is often referred to as the "Hebrew Bible." Parts of
Daniel and Ezra, plus one verse in Jeremiah and two words in Genesis (a proper name), are in Aramaic, which is to classical Hebrew
more or less what contemporary English is to Chaucer. Most scholars would agree that many if not all of the Old Testament books
reached their final form through a process of editing. This may
have been going on over many centuries, and may have involved
considerable fresh writing. However, several books of which this is
likely to be true (for example, the prophet Isaiah) retain a remarkable inner coherence. Our knowledge of the original text of the
Old Testament has been enormously enriched by the discovery
of the Dead Sea Scrolls, documents thought to have been written in the last two centuries BC. They include copies of most of the
Old Testament books, and show that the much later manuscripts
upon which mainstream Judaism and Christianity have depended
are very close, despite small variations, to the texts that would have
been known in Jesus's day.

Over the two hundred years or so before the time of Jesus, all these books were translated into Greek, probably in Egypt, for the benefit of the increasing number of Jews for whom Greek was the primary language. The Greek Bible they produced was, in various different versions, the one used by most early Christians. It is known as the "Septuagint" (from the Latin for "seventy") because of stories about there having been seventy translators.

This is the point in history at which the books which came to be known as "Apocrypha" (literally, "hidden things") first appeared. A long and complex debate about their status and validity rumbled on in the early church, reemerging in the sixteenth and seventeenth centuries. As a result of that debate, some Bibles include the Apocrypha and some don't. Those that do include them normally print the relevant books (sometimes adding some extra ones as well) in between the Old and the New Testaments, though the so-called Jerusalem Bible and other official Roman Catholic publications treat the Apocrypha simply as part of the Old Testament. Sadly, more people today are vaguely aware that these books have been controversial than have ever read them for themselves. At the very least, these books (like other works of the period, such as the Dead Sea Scrolls and the writings of Josephus) tell us a great deal about how Jews of the time of Jesus thought and lived. Some of the books, such as the Wisdom of Solomon, provide significant partial parallels, and possibly even sources, for some of the ideas in the New Testament, not least in the writings of Paul.

The twenty-seven books of the New Testament were all written within two generations of the time of Jesus—in other words, by the end of the first century at the latest—though most scholars would put most of them earlier than that. The letters of Paul are from the late forties and the fifties, and though disputes continue as to whether he wrote all the letters that bear his name, they are the first written testimony to the explosive events of Jesus himself and the very early church.

We looked in Chapter Seven at the current debates surrounding the gospels, and I made it clear that I saw no reason to suppose that books such as the Gospel of Thomas—books sometimes called "the apocryphal New Testament"—were even close to the canonical material in age, or for that matter in substance. The significance of the books in this category consists not so much in their witness to Jesus himself, as in the evidence they provide for the thought and practice of a later period.

By contrast, the four gospels, Acts, and the thirteen letters ascribed to Paul were regarded as authentic and authoritative from very early on—by the early to middle second century at the latest. Doubts persisted about some books, such as Hebrews, Revelation, and some of the smaller letters. Some individual churches and teachers in the second and third centuries regarded other books as authoritative, such as the Letter of Barnabas and the Shepherd of Hermas (both included in what are now known as the "Apostolic Fathers," a collection of very early Christian writings readily available in modern translations). Most early Christians, though, while valuing these writings in themselves, didn't see them as on the same level as the works they saw as "apostolic," and thus carrying a badge of authenticity.

It needs to be stressed that our evidence for the text of the New Testament is in a completely different league than our evidence for every single other book from the ancient world. We know major Greek authors such as Plato and Sophocles, and even Homer, through a small handful of manuscripts, many of them medieval. We know Roman authors such as Tacitus and Pliny through similarly few copies—in some cases just one or two, and many of them again very late. By contrast, we possess literally hundreds of early manuscripts of some or all of the New Testament, putting us in an unrivaled position to work back from the small variations which creep into any manuscript tradition and discern the likely original text. (When I say "early," by the way, I mean from the first six or seven centuries, which is many centuries earlier than the oldest surviving manuscripts of most classical authors. We have dozens of New Testament manuscripts from the third and fourth centuries, and a few from as early as the second.) Yes, scribes may have introduced alterations here and there. But the massive evidence available means that we are on extremely secure ground for getting at what the biblical authors actually wrote.

Pressure on the church to firm up its list of authoritative books didn't come, as is sometimes said today, from a desire to present a socially or politically acceptable theology; these debates were going on through periods of fierce, if intermittent, persecution. Rather, the impetus came from those who offered rival "canons." Some of these cut out key passages from the main books, as was done by Marcion, a Roman teacher in the second century. Others added new books with different teachings, as was done by the Gnostics, as part of their claim to possess secret teachings of what Jesus and the apostles "really" said.

For much of church history, the churches of the East read the Bible in Greek, and the churches of the West, Latin. One of the great slogans of the sixteenth-century Reformation was that the Bible should be available to all people in their own language, a principle which is now more or less universally acknowledged across the whole Christian world. This precipitated a flurry of translating activity in the sixteenth century itself, led by the German Reformer Martin Luther and the Englishman William Tyndale. Things then settled down by the seventeenth century, with the English-speaking world adopting the Authorized ("King James") Version in 1611, and remaining content with it for nearly three hundred years thereafter. As more and better new manuscripts were discovered, revealing all kinds of mostly small but interesting adjustments that needed to be made, scholars and church leaders in the late nineteenth century were persuaded that further revision was advisable. This opened the floodgates again, and the last hundred years have seen a further flurry of translations and revisions, with literally dozens now available. Similar stories can be told of translations in other languages. Organizations such as the Bible Society and the Wycliffe Bible Translators have worked tirelessly to render scripture into more and more of the world's native languages. The task is enormous, but the church has for many generations now seen it as a priority.

This story of the Bible's composition, collection, and distribution has to be told. But setting it out in this way feels a bit like trying to describe my best friend by offering a biochemical analysis of his genetic makeup. That technical information is important. Indeed, if he didn't have his particular genetic makeup he wouldn't be the same person. But there's something vital missing. It's that extra *je ne sais quoi* for which we shall now hunt.

God's Inspired Word

Why is the Bible important? Most Christians down the years have said something at this point about it being *inspired*. What might this mean?

People have meant a variety of different things by that description. Sometimes they have really meant not inspired, but inspir*ing*: this book, they find, breathes new life into them. (The "-spired" bit of the word "inspired" means, literally, "breathed.") More often, though, they've meant an older meaning of the word "inspired." In that sense the word isn't talking about the effect something has on us. It's talking about something that's true of the thing in itself.

At that level, people sometimes say "the sunset was inspired," meaning (presumably) that it carried a special quality which seemed to set it apart from more mundane evenings. In the same way, people talk of a piece of music, a play, or a dance as being "inspired." But the sunset, and even the most sublime symphony, is part of the general order of creation. If the point of calling the Bible "inspired" is to say, "It's a bit like Shakespeare or Homer," that doesn't get at what's normally meant by "the inspiration of scripture." People who intend that sort of general-order-of-creation comparison are, perhaps deliberately, putting the biblical "inspiration" into something like the worldview of Option One.

Sometimes people take this tack to avoid Option Two, which sees "the inspiration of scripture" as an act of pure "supernatural" intervention, bypassing the minds of the writers altogether. In a strict version of Option Two, no divine inspiration would be possible, of course, since God and the world—including human beings—live in different spheres, with a great gulf between them. But many who have insisted on the Bible's inspiration have tried to do so within this framework, envisaging God either dictating books from a great distance or "zapping" the writers with some kind of long-range linguistic thunderbolt. I suspect that many who have reacted against the idea that the Bible is actually "inspired" in some full and rich sense are really trying to rule out that kind of statement of the idea, with all the oddities that it seems to entail. Who can blame them? After all, a glance at Paul, or Jeremiah, or Hosea is enough to indicate just how much the personality of the writer is alive and well and energetically visible within the text.

Once again Option Three comes to the rescue. Supposing scripture, like the sacraments, is one of the points where heaven and earth overlap and interlock? Like all other such places, this is mysterious. It doesn't mean we can see at once what's going on. Indeed, it guarantees that we can't. But it does enable us to say some things that need to be said and that are otherwise difficult.

In particular, it enables us to say that the writers, compilers, editors, and even collectors of scripture were people who, with different personalities, styles, methods, and intentions, were nonetheless caught up in the strange purposes of the covenant God—purposes which included the communication, by writing, of his word. It enables us to speak about God the creator (the one we know supremely through the living Word, Jesus) being himself (so to speak) a wordsmith. Option Three enables us to insist that, though words are not the only thing God specializes in, they are a central part of his repertoire. It also helps us to see that when this God is going to work within his world, he wants to work through his image-bearing human creatures, and that, since he wants to do so as far as possible with their intelligent cooperation, he wants to communicate with and through them verbally—in addition to, but also as a central point within, his many other ways of getting things said and done.

The Bible is far more, in other words, than what some people used to say a generation or so ago: that it was simply the (or a) "record of the revelation," as though God revealed himself by some quite other means and the Bible was simply what people wrote down to remind themselves of what had happened. The Bible offers itself, and has normally been treated in the church, as part of God's revelation, not simply a witness or echo of it. Part of the problem is the assumption that what's required is after all simply "revelation," the communication of some kind of true information. The Bible does indeed offer plenty of information, but what it offers in a more primary way is energy for the task to which God is calling his people. Talking about the inspiration of the Bible is one way of saying that that energy comes from the work of God's Spirit.

It helps, in all this, to remind ourselves constantly what the Bible is given to us *for*. One of the most famous statements of "inspiration" in the Bible itself puts it like this: "All scripture is inspired by God and is useful for teaching, for reproof, for correction, and for training in righteousness, so that everyone who belongs to God may be proficient, equipped for every good work" (2 Timothy 3:16–17). *Equipped for every good work;* there's the point. The Bible is breathed out by God (the word for "inspired" in this case is *theopneustos*—literally, "God-breathed") so that it can fashion and form God's people to do his work in the world.

In other words, the Bible isn't there simply to be an accurate reference point for people who want to look things up and be sure they've got them right. It is there to equip God's people to carry forward his purposes of new covenant and new creation. It is there to enable people to work for justice, to sustain their spirituality as they do so, to create and enhance relationships at every level, and to produce that new creation which will have about it something of the beauty of God himself. The Bible isn't like an accurate description of how a car is made. It's more like the mechanic who helps you fix it, the garage attendant who refuels it, and the guide who tells you how to get where you're going. And where you're going is *to make God's new creation happen in his world,* not simply to find your own way unscathed through the old creation.

That is why, though I'm not unhappy with what people are trying to affirm when they use words like "infallible" (the idea that the Bible won't deceive us) and "inerrant" (the stronger idea, that the Bible can't get things wrong), I normally resist using those words myself. Ironically, in my experience, debates about words like these have often led people away from the Bible itself and into all kinds of theories which do no justice to scripture as a whole— its great story, its larger purposes, its sustained climax, its haunting sense of an unfinished novel beckoning us to become, in our own right, characters in its closing episodes. Instead, the insistence on an "infallible" or "inerrant" Bible has grown up within a complex cultural matrix (that, in particular, of modern North American Protestantism) where the Bible has been seen as the bastion of orthodoxy against Roman Catholicism on the one hand and liberal modernism on the other. Unfortunately, the assumptions of both those worlds have conditioned the debate. It is no accident that this Protestant insistence on biblical infallibility arose at the same time that Rome was insisting on papal infallibility, or that the rationalism of the Enlightenment infected even those who were battling against it.

Such debates, in my view, distract attention from the real point of what the Bible is there for. (I am reminded of a legend about Karl Barth. On being asked by a woman whether the serpent in Genesis actually spoke, he replied, "Madam, it doesn't matter whether the serpent spoke. What matters is *what the serpent said.*") Squabbling over particular definitions of the qualities of the Bible is like a married couple squabbling over which of them loves the children more, when they should be getting on with bringing them up and setting them a good example. The Bible is there to enable God's people to be equipped to do God's work in God's world, not to give them an excuse to sit back smugly, knowing they possess all God's truth.

Fourteen

The Story and the Task

One of the things Christians regularly say about the Bible is that it's "authoritative." But what we might mean by this has become difficult to grasp.

One excellent place to begin is with something Jesus himself said about the nature of authority. Pagan rulers, he said, lord it over their subjects, but it mustn't be like that with you. Anyone who wants to be first must be the servant of all, because the Son of Man didn't come to be served, but to serve, and to give his life as a ransom for many (Mark 10:35–45). If God's authority is vested in Jesus, and if the Bible derives such authority as it has from that same divine source, what we're saying by calling the Bible "authoritative" is that the Bible, somehow, becomes *an authoritative instrument of what God accomplished through Jesus—particularly through his death and resurrection.*

In other words, for Jesus's death to have the effect it was intended to have, it must be communicated to the world through the "word" of the gospel. (As we saw in Chapter Ten, God's "word," for the early Christians, was the powerful proclamation of Jesus's lordship.) And the Bible, in setting out the roots of the Christian story in the Old Testament and its full flowering in the New, was seen from very early on as encapsulating that powerful word—the word which communicated, and so put into effect, what God accomplished in Jesus. The Bible, in fact, is not simply an *authoritative description of* a saving plan, as though it were just an aerial photograph of a particular piece of landscape. It is *part of the saving plan itself.* It is more like the guide who takes you around the landscape and shows you how you can enjoy it to the full.

That is why the Bible's "authority" works in an altogether different way from the "authority" of, say, the rules of a golf club. The Bible does indeed contain lists of rules (the Ten Commandments, for instance, in Exodus 20), but as it stands, as a whole, it doesn't consist of a list of dos and don'ts. It's a *story,* a grand, epic narrative that runs from the Garden of Eden, where Adam and Eve look after the animals, to the city which is the Bride of the Lamb, out of which the water of life flows to refresh the world. It is, after all, a love story, albeit with a difference. And the authority of the Bible is the authority of a love story in which we are invited to take part. It is, in that sense, more like the "authority" of a dance in which we are invited to join; or of a novel in which, though the scene is set, the plot well developed, and the ending planned and in sight, there is still some way to go, and we are invited to become living, participating, intelligent, and decision-making characters within the story as it moves toward its destination.

This model of "authority" helps us to understand how to read the Bible as Christian scripture. The "authority" of the Old Testament is precisely the "authority" possessed by an *earlier* scene in the novel—when we are now living in a *later* scene. It matters that the earlier scene was what it was. But it has done its job and taken us to the later scene, where some things have changed quite radically. The plot has moved forward. Even in the most postmodern of novels, characters in the final chapters don't normally repeat what they said and did near the beginning.

This doesn't mean that we are left in a free-for-all situation where it's open to anyone to say, "Well, we're now at a new moment in God's plan, so we can throw away anything we don't like in the old moments." It is still the same story; and that story was, and is, the story of how the creator God is rescuing the creation from its rebellion, brokenness, corruption, and death. He has accomplished this through the death and resurrection of Jesus the Messiah, in fulfillment of the promises to, and the story of, Israel. All that is non-negotiable. Anything that contradicts or undermines that doesn't take the novel forward to its intended conclusion. Paul argues like this again and again throughout his letters, and we must be prepared to do the same.

Living with "the authority of scripture," then, means living in the world of the story which scripture tells. It means soaking ourselves in that story, as a community and as individuals. Indeed, it means that Christian leaders and teachers must themselves become part of the process, part of the way in which God is at work not only *in* the Bible-reading community but *through* that community in and for the wider world. That is the way to become surefooted in our proposal of, or reflection upon, fresh initiatives or suggestions about how the Christian community should respond to new situations— for instance, in spotting that what the world now needs, in fulfillment of some of scripture's deepest plans, is global economic justice. It means being, as a community, so attentive not just to what our traditions say about scripture, but to scripture itself, that we are able, by means of it, to live by the life of heaven even while on earth.

All this means that we are called to be people who learn to hear God's voice speaking today within the ancient text, and who become vessels of that living word in the world around us.

Listening for God's Voice

God does indeed speak through scripture: both to the church and, God willing, *through* the church to the world. Both of these are important. We can understand this idea if we place it within the now familiar notion of the overlap of heaven and earth, and of the way in which God's future purposes, having come forward to meet us in Jesus, are now to be implemented ahead of the day when God makes all things new.

Reading scripture, like praying and sharing in the sacraments, is one of the means by which the life of heaven and the life of earth interlock. (This is what older writers were referring to when they spoke of "the means of grace." It isn't that we can control God's grace, but that there are, so to speak, places to go where God has promised to meet with his people, even if sometimes when we turn up it feels as though God has forgotten the date. More usually it's the other way around.) We read scripture in order to hear God addressing us—*us,* here and now, today.

How this happens is unpredictable and often mysterious. *That* it happens is the testimony of millions of Christians through the centuries. Techniques have been developed to facilitate our hearing God's voice in scripture, and many of them are helpful (schemes of private reading, for example, to enable people to work systematically through the Bible over a period of a year, or three years, or whatever, without getting indigestion by trying to read all four gospels on top of one another, or all of Leviticus and Numbers at a run). Whole systems of spirituality have grown up around the prayerful reading of scripture. Within evangelicalism, the "quiet time" of reading scripture and listening for the voice of God has been central; many evangelicals are surprised to discover that St. Benedict and some other Roman Catholic teachers have developed a very similar system, known as *lectio divina.* Within some such meditative methods, readers seek prayerfully to "become" a character in the story they are reading, and then to watch and wait, as the story unfolds, to see what will be said to them, or even required of them. And of course, throughout the history of the church, preachers have sought both to understand what scripture was saying in its original context and to convey to their hearers what this might mean in their own day. Indeed, it wouldn't be going too far to say that this is the backbone of what Christian preaching is all about.

The dangers are obvious, and no techniques will succeed in eliminating them; nor should they, because in doing so they might quench the Spirit altogether. The way in which we "hear" scripture, and thereby hear God's voice speaking to us through scripture, is bound up with all kinds of "subjective" factors. None the worse for that, of course. If it isn't subjective, it isn't, in that sense, real for us. But hearing God's voice in scripture isn't simply a matter of precise, technical expertise. It's a matter of love—which, as I have already hinted, is the mode of knowing required for living at the intersection between heaven and earth. But because our love remains frail and partial, and because in the nature of the case our own hopes and fears are so closely bound up with it, our hearing of God's voice as we read scripture always needs testing by reference to other fellow Christians, past as well as present, and indeed other scriptural passages themselves. That's just common sense. Listening to God's voice in scripture doesn't put us in the position of having infallible opinions. It puts us where it put Jesus himself: in possession of a vocation, whether for a lifetime or for the next minute. Vocations are fragile, and are tested in performance. That is what it's like to live at the intersection of heaven and earth.

But the performance isn't just about our own private pilgrimage. It's about becoming agents of God's new world—workers for justice, explorers of spirituality, makers and menders of relationships, creators of beauty. If God does indeed speak through scripture, he speaks in order to commission us for tasks like these. Christian scripture is stamped, in its shape and overall purpose and mode of use as well as in its individual parts, not only with the coming together of heaven and earth, but with the overlap and interplay of present and future. It's a book designed to be read by those who are living in the present in the light of God's future—the future which has arrived in Jesus and now demands to be implemented.

All this means that the Christian scriptures, just like Christian prayer, have their own distinctive shape. Reading them in the way they seem to intend and require is likewise a distinctive kind of activity. This needs unpacking a bit further.

Not all "holy books" are the same *sort* of thing. The great writings of the Hindu tradition—the Bhagavad Gita, in particular—do not offer a controlling story within which the readers are summoned to become characters. They do not speak of a single god who, as the unique creator, chooses to act in one specific family and location rather than all others in order thereby to address the whole world. This affects form as well as content. The Koran, the majestic monument to Muhammad, is a different sort of thing again, much more like (in fact) the kind of hard-edged "authoritative" book which some would consider the Bible to be—or perhaps we should say into which they would like to turn the Bible. Even Judaism, whose Bible the church has made its own, doesn't tell a continuing story of the Christian sort, a story in which the readers are summoned to become fresh characters. The place taken by Jesus within Christianity is taken in Judaism by, if anything, the further codifications and discussions of the Torah found in the Mishnah and the Talmud, though there again we find an obvious difference of shape and aim as well as of content.

This doesn't mean that the God who is the Lord of all creation as well as the God of Abraham, Isaac, and Jacob has nothing to say through anyone else's scriptures. It means, rather, that what the Christian believes about Jesus generates a narrative within which one is called to live; that living within that story generates a call to a particular vocation within the world; and that the Bible is the book through which God sustains and directs those who seek to obey that vocation as intelligent, thinking, image-bearing human beings. The Bible constantly challenges its readers not to rest content. Giving the church such a gift was a way of pointing out to each generation that we need to grow up, to become more fully human, in our thinking. That is done not least through God's addressing us in words—words which force us either to retreat into shallow, shoulder-shrugging denial or to think more deeply, to work out what he is up to and what he wants of us. More particularly, what he wants to do *through* us. Scripture is there to enable us to glimpse the task before us and to become the sort of people through whom that task can be attempted and accomplished.

The Challenge of Interpretation

How then is scripture to be interpreted? In a sense, the whole present book is an answer to that question. A fuller answer would insist that we take account of the nature of each book, each chapter, each syllable. Contexts, meanings within particular cultures, the overall place of a book, a theme, a line within that culture and time and within the scope and sweep of scripture itself—all these things matter. Exploring them with the rigor and attention they deserve constitutes a massive task, though there are today all kinds of encouragements and helps in undertaking it.

But the main things to recognize are that God intends that we should have this book and should read and study it, individually and corporately; and that this book, by the power of the Spirit, bears witness in a thousand ways to Jesus himself, and to what God has accomplished through him. To repeat a point I made earlier, but a vital one: the Bible isn't simply a repository of true information about God, Jesus, and the hope of the world. It is, rather, part of *the means by which,* in the power of the Spirit, the living God rescues his people and his world, and takes them forward on the journey toward his new creation, and makes us agents of that new creation even as we travel.

But what about the phrase one hears whenever the Bible is discussed both in church circles and in the wider world? "It all depends," said a reporter on the news just a few nights ago, "whether people are reading the Bible literally or seeing that it needs to be interpreted." Or, as I recently heard a lecturer assert with great emphasis, "Some people take the Bible literally, while others of us see it as metaphorical." What does it mean to "take the Bible literally"? What would it mean to read it "metaphorically"? Is this even a helpful way of putting the question?

Broadly speaking: no, it isn't. The old distinction between "literal" and "metaphorical" needs to be shaken up a bit, for a start, before we can do anything useful with it.

Ironically, considering what they mean, the words "literal" and "literally" have come to be used in a variety of slippery ways. Often "literally" actually means "metaphorically," as when a sunbather reports, "My arms were literally on fire after sitting there all afternoon," or an office worker says, "The phone has literally not stopped ringing all day." Sometimes it simply means "really, truly," when in fact tacitly acknowledging that what is said is neither real nor true: "My boss is literally an Adolf Hitler."

But when it's used in relation to the Bible, it raises echoes of one controversy in particular: the interpretation of the creation story in Genesis. Nobody in America will need reminding of the polarized debates between those who insisted, and still insist, on a literal seven-day creation, and those who insisted, and still insist, on a rereading of Genesis 1 in the light of evolutionary science. The debate that has been conducted in terms of "creation versus evolution" has gotten caught up with all kinds of other debates (in American culture in particular), and this has provided a singularly unhelpful backdrop to the would-be serious discussion of other parts of the Bible.

In fact, every Bible reader I've ever met, from whatever background or culture, has known instinctively that at least some parts of the Bible are meant literally and other parts are meant metaphorically. When the Old Testament declares that the Babylonians captured Jerusalem and burned it down, it means, quite literally, that they captured Jerusalem and burned it down. When Paul says that he was shipwrecked three times, he means that he was shipwrecked three times. On the other hand, when he says that a thief will come in the night, so that the pregnant woman will go into labor, so that you mustn't fall asleep or get drunk, but must stay awake and put on your armor (1 Thessalonians 5:1–8), it would take a particularly inept reader not to recognize one of his most spectacular mixed metaphors. And when the messenger of the Assyrian king shouts to Hezekiah's men that Egypt is "a broken reed, which will pierce the hand of anyone who leans on it" (2 Kings 18:21), the fact that reeds grow in Egypt and that the metaphor might be quite appropriate is unlikely to blind us to the fact that it is indeed a metaphor.

Other obvious examples include the parables of Jesus. I've never yet met a reader who was under the impression that the story of the prodigal son had actually happened, so that if you visited enough family farms around Palestine you would eventually run into the old father and his two sons (always supposing they'd made up their quarrel). Virtually all readers negotiate this point without even thinking about it. Jesus himself sometimes emphasized it (not that his hearers were likely to be mistaken on the matter) by pointing out "literal" meanings ("Go," he said, "and do likewise" [Luke 10.37]). Sometimes the gospel writers did the same, as when Mark said that the priests realized that a particular parable was aimed against them (12:12). But this doesn't mean that the only "truth" in the parables is the point at which they can be, so to speak, cashed out. The parables are "true" at several quite different levels; and to recognize this is *not* a way of saying, "The only real 'truths' that matter are the 'spiritual' meanings, the things that didn't 'happen' as events in the real world." Truth (thank God) is more complicated than that, because God's world is more complicated—more interesting, in fact—than that.

Another problem, a source of endless confusion, emerges at this point. In addition to the casual use of "literally" I mentioned a moment ago, people today use the words "literally" and "metaphorically" to mean two different sorts of things. On the one hand, and in accordance with the true meaning of the two words, they refer to *the way words refer to things.* "Father" means, literally, someone who begets a child. "A rose" refers, literally, to the flower of that name. But if I were to say to my granddaughter, "You're my little rose," I would be denoting a person but referring metaphorically to a flower, in order to invest the former with some of the attributes of the latter (pretty, fresh, and sweet-smelling; not, I trust, prickly). And when a devout parishioner refers to a priest as "Father," we assume that the reference is straightforwardly metaphorical, investing the man with paternal qualities which have nothing to do with actually begetting children. Here, the words "literal" and "metaphorical" aren't telling us whether the things I'm talking about are abstract or concrete, but whether the words "Father" and "rose" are being used literally, to refer to an actual father and an actual rose, or metaphorically, to refer (not to an abstract entity, but) to actual persons who are not, in fact, fathers or roses but whom we understand better by, as it were, draping those words for a moment around their necks.

But "literal" and "metaphorical" have come to mean, as well, something to do with *the sort of things we are referring to.* "Was it a literal resurrection, or a metaphorical one?" We all know what the speaker is asking: Did it actually happen, or not? But using "literal" and "metaphorical" in this way, however common it may be, is deeply confusing. It makes the word "literal" do duty for "concrete," and "metaphorical" either for "abstract" or for some other nonconcrete idea ("spiritual," perhaps, though that introduces a host of further confusions).

This is only the tip of the iceberg of the discussion that we could have at this point, but there are two things I want to stress. First, we shouldn't allow the backdrop of older, unhelpful debates about Genesis to fool us into thinking that anyone who insists that some historical part of the Bible is to be read literally, and that it intends to denote things that actually happened in concrete reality, is to be taken as a simpleton who hasn't learned either to read texts or to live in today's real world. Nor should we allow the same polarization to make us imagine that someone who insists on reading the Bible's splendid metaphors *as* metaphors—for instance, reading "the Son of Man coming on the clouds" as a metaphor indicating vindication and exaltation—is a dangerous antiliteralist who has given up believing in the truth of Christianity.

The Bible is full of passages which really do intend to describe things that happened in the real world—and, for that matter, to command and forbid various types of actions which occur in the real world. The God of whom the Bible speaks is, after all, the creator of that world. Part of the point of the whole story is that he loves that world and intends to rescue it, that he's put his plan into operation through a series of concrete events in actual history, and that he intends this plan to be worked out through the concrete lives and work of his people. But the Bible, like virtually all other great writing, regularly and repeatedly brings out the flavor, the meaning, the proper interpretation of these actual, concrete, space-time events by means of complex, beautiful, and evocative literary forms and figures, of which metaphor is only one. Acknowledging (indeed, celebrating) the intended literal reference, investigating the concrete events thus referred to, and exploring the full range of metaphorical meaning—these tasks are to be integrated together as key elements of biblical interpretation.

The second thing I want to stress is that it is then open to any reader, commentator, or preacher to explore, in a particular passage, which bits are "meant literally," which bits are "meant metaphorically," and which bits might have been meant both ways—before turning, as a second stage, to ask whether the bits which were "meant literally" actually happened in concrete reality. This simply can't be decided in advance by insisting either that "everything in the Bible must be taken literally" or that we know in advance that most of it "should be taken metaphorically."

Take the example of the "Son of Man" passage I referred to a moment ago, which comes from Daniel 7. The passage speaks of Daniel having a dream in which four monsters, "beasts," come up out of the sea. Now for a start, although it is quite possible that the passage goes back to an actual person called Daniel who had strange turbulent dreams and longed to interpret them, the book is closely related to a well-known genre that uses the conscious and deliberate construction of fictitious "dreams" for the purpose of extended allegory. (Think of John Bunyan's *Pilgrim's Progress.*) That is a possibility we should at least hold open.

Beyond that, the four "beasts"—the lion, the leopard, the bear, and the final monster with ten horns—are manifestly metaphorical. Nobody in the ancient world, or I think the modern, if asked whether Daniel's dream had come true, would investigate whether such animals "really existed"—whether you could go and see them in the wild, or in a zoo. But the fact that there were four of them was meant quite literally. It was read that way by ancient Jews (who calculated in fear and trembling where they were in the sequence), and it's read that way by all modern commentators. The interesting observation that the fourth beast was almost certainly understood in the second century BC as referring to Syria, and in the first century AD as referring to Rome, merely serves to underline the fact that the metaphorical language intended a literal reference to concrete reality, even though different generations differed as to what that literal referent, that concrete reality, might be.

Again, when the dream says that the monsters "come up out of the sea" (7:2), we don't regard it as a contradiction when the angel who interprets the dream says that "four kings shall arise out of the earth" (7:17). Many ancient Jews regarded the sea as the place and source of chaos; and part of the point of Daniel 7 (ironically, in view of where this discussion began) is to interpret Genesis 1, with life emerging from the sea and a human being eventually bringing God's order to it all. The kings come metaphorically "from the sea"; but they are concrete kings with real-life land-based armies, not abstract entities or ideas in people's minds. And the "coming of the Son of Man" in 7:13 is interpreted, not in the literal terms of a human figure flying around on a cloud, but in the metaphorical but thoroughly concrete terms of "the holy ones of the Most High" (that is, loyal Jews) "receiving the kingdom and possessing it forever and ever" (7:18).

All this is a way of saying: the polarization between "literal" and "metaphorical" interpretation has become confused and confusing. People who find themselves getting trapped in it should take a deep breath, read some of the Bible's glorious metaphors, think about the concrete events that the writers were referring to, and begin again.

We should take particular care to avoid one subtle but powerful line of thought. It is all too easy to suppose that, if the Bible is not really "to be taken literally," but mostly to be interpreted "metaphorically," the writers (and perhaps even God) are not really interested in what we do with our own concrete circumstances, our bodily and economic and political life. Saying "metaphorical, not literal" can lead quite quickly into the suggestion, all the more powerful for it's never quite being stated head on, that God only really cares about our nonconcrete ("spiritual") life, thoughts, and feelings. As soon as we find that nonsense coming up out of the sea, we should recognize it. It is the monstrous, dualistic lie which half our culture has embraced, and which the whole Bible, read literally, metaphorically, and every other way you can think of, ought to defeat and destroy. No first-century Jew would have thought like that. Nor would any early Christian either.

The interpretation of the Bible remains, then, a huge and wonderful task. That is why we need to engage in it as far as we have time and ability. We must do this not only individually, but also through careful and prayerful study within the life of the church, where different members will have different skills and knowledge to help. The only sure rule is to remember that the Bible is indeed God's gift to the church, to equip that church for its work in the world, and that serious study of it can and should become one of the places where, and the means by which, heaven and earth interlock and God's future purposes arrive in the present. The Bible is part of God's answer to the ancient human quest for justice, spirituality, relationship, and beauty. Read it and see.

✝

Fifteen

Believing and Belonging

The river and the tree appear to be opposites.

The river begins, quite literally, all over the place. A tiny spring way up in the hills; a distant lake, itself fed by streams; a melting glacier—all of them and a thousand more contribute to the babble and rush of water, the smooth flow here and the swirling rapids there. Gradually other streams, other whole rivers, make their contribution. Out of many there emerges the one. I lived for a time by the banks of the Ottawa River in Canada, just upstream from where it joins the St. Lawrence. It is, at that point, over a mile wide. Many streams have made it what it is.

The tree begins with a single seed. An acorn or its equivalent falls into the earth: tiny, vulnerable, alone. It germinates and puts out roots down into the dark earth. Simultaneously it sends up a shoot into the light and air. The roots quickly diverge and probe all over the place, looking for nourishment and water. The shoot becomes a trunk, again a single upright stalk, but this, too, quickly diverges. An oak or a cedar will spread far and wide in all directions. Even the tall, narrow poplar is far more than just a single trunk. The river flows from many into one; the tree grows from one into many.

We need both images if we are to understand the church.

The church is like a river. In the last book of the Bible, John the visionary sees a huge throng of people from every nation, kindred, tribe, and tongue coming together in a great chorus of praise.

Like the river, they all started in different places, but they have now brought their different streams into a single flow. The image of the river reminds us forcibly that, though the church consists by definition of people from the widest possible variety of backgrounds, part of the point of it all is that they belong to one another, and are meant to be part of the same powerful flow, going now in the same single direction. Diversity gives way to unity.

But at the same time the church is like a tree. The single seed, Jesus himself, has been sown in the dark earth and has produced an amazing plant. Branches have set off in all directions, some pointing almost directly upward, some reaching down to the earth, some heading out over neighboring walls. Looking at the eager, outstretched branches, you'd hardly know they were all from the same stem. But they are. Unity generates diversity.

These images shouldn't be pressed too far. In the final chapter of the Bible, where river and trees come together as part of the extraordinary picture of the New Jerusalem, the river comes from a single source, and the trees all bear leaves with the same healing power. But this double image nonetheless helps us understand something of what Christians mean by the church—the people of God, the Body of Christ, the Bride of Christ, God's household, the motley collection of people who gather periodically in the shabby building up the road. What is the church? Who belongs to it, and how? Equally to the point, what is the church *for*?

The Church and Its Purpose

The church is the single, multiethnic family promised by the creator God to Abraham. It was brought into being through Israel's Messiah, Jesus; it was energized by God's Spirit; and it was called to bring the transformative news of God's rescuing justice to the whole creation. That's a tightly packed definition, and every bit of it matters. Let's look at it more closely and see how both the river and the tree contribute to our understanding.

First, the church is the single great river formed from tens of thousands of scattered tributaries. Even when, in the days of the early Israelites, it was mostly a single family, there was plenty of room for outsiders (such as Ruth, in the book that bears her name) to come in to the one family of Israel. Once Jesus had done what he did, that became the new norm: people of every race, every geographical and cultural background, every shape, sort, and size were summoned and welcomed into this renewed people. Calling the church "the people of God" picks up this idea of the continuity, stressed throughout earliest Christianity, between the family of Abraham and the worldwide family of the church. Perhaps the main problem with this image, taken by itself, is that it leaves us (as it left the early Christians) with the puzzle of why so many Jews, right from the start, didn't believe that Jesus was their Messiah and so didn't come to belong to the family that hailed him as Lord.

Second, the church is the many-branched tree planted by God when he called Abraham: the tree whose single trunk is Jesus, and whose many branches, twigs, leaves, and so on are the millions of Christian communities and Christian individuals around the world. One central biblical way of saying much the same thing is to follow Paul and think of the church as the "Body of Christ," the single body in which every individual, and every local community, is a limb or an organ. "The body" is more than merely an image of unity-in-diversity; it's a way of saying that the church is called to *do* the work of Christ, to be the means of his *action* in and for the world. The tree, rooted in ancient Israel, standing up straight in Jesus, branching out with his life in all directions, is to be the means of implementing his work, of making his achievement real in all the world. Looking at the church this way is very close to another biblical image, one which we find both in the Old Testament and in Jesus's own teaching: God's people as the vine, a single plant with many branches.

In both of these images the idea of "family" is never far away, but it can be misleading. At one level it's central; the early Christians did their best to live as an extended family, caring for each other in the way in which (in that world) extended families did. They called each other "brother" and "sister" and really meant it. They lived and prayed and thought like that: children of the same father, following the same older brother, sharing goods and resources where need arose. When they talked about "love," that's the main thing they meant: living as a single family, a mutually supporting community. The church must never forget that calling.

But at the same time the idea of "family" can take us in the wrong direction. As many preachers have said (I've heard it attributed to Billy Graham, among others), God has no grandchildren. One of the biggest battles in the early church was all about whether people coming in from the outside, into what was still basically a Jewish community, had to become Jews—that is, had to go through the process of becoming a "proselyte"—in order to belong to the people of God as redefined around Jesus. (This would have meant that they had to practice the Jewish Law, including having their menfolk circumcised.) The answer, from Paul and the rest, was a resounding no. God welcomes non-Jews as non-Jews, and doesn't require them to become Jewish. At the same time, Jews themselves couldn't rely on their birth and ancestral status to assure themselves that they were automatically members in the renewed family which God was creating through the Messiah. As John the Baptist had said, the ax is laid to the roots of the tree.

Nor does a person belong to the Messiah and his people simply because of being born into a Christian family or household. That's not to deny that families have played a significant part in the development of the church. Many of the earliest Christians were related to one another. Sometimes two or three families have contributed massively to the life and work of the church in particular areas and generations. But, as we all know, it's perfectly possible for someone to grow up in a Christian household and turn his or her back on its faith and life; and it's not only possible but gloriously and frequently real that people who grew up having no contact with the gospel or the church come into full and active membership. Many branches fall off the tree; many streams come together into the single river. Being born into a particular human family doesn't determine whether or not you will become a member of the family of God.

Many people today find it difficult to grasp this sense of corporate Christian identity. We have been so soaked in the individualism of modern Western culture that we feel threatened by the idea of our primary identity being that of the family we belong to—especially when the family in question is so large, stretching across space and time. The church isn't simply a collection of isolated individuals, all following their own pathways of spiritual growth without much reference to one another. It may sometimes look like that, and even feel like that. And it's gloriously true that each of us is called to respond to God's call at a personal level. You can hide in the shadows at the back of the church for a while, but sooner or later you have to decide whether this is for you or not. But we need to learn again the lesson (to take St. Paul's image of the Body of Christ) that a hand is no less a hand for being part of a larger whole, an entire body. The foot is not diminished in its freedom to be a foot by being part of a body which also contains eyes and ears. In fact, hands and feet are most free to be themselves when they coordinate properly with eyes, ears, and everything else. Cutting them off in an effort to make them truly free, truly themselves, would be truly disastrous.

In particular, it would deny the very purpose for which the church was called into being. According to the early Christians, the church doesn't exist in order to provide a place where people can pursue their private spiritual agendas and develop their own spiritual potential. Nor does it exist in order to provide a safe haven in which people can hide from the wicked world and ensure that they themselves arrive safely at an otherworldly destination. Private spiritual growth and ultimate salvation come rather as the by-products of the main, central, overarching purpose for which God has called and is calling us. This purpose is clearly stated in various places in the New Testament: that through the church God will announce to the wider world that he is indeed its wise, loving, and just creator; that through Jesus he has defeated the powers that corrupt and enslave it; and that by his Spirit he is at work to heal and renew it.

The church exists, in other words, for what we sometimes call "mission": to announce to the world that Jesus is its Lord. This is the "good news," and when it's announced it transforms people and societies. Mission, in its widest as well as its more focused senses, is what the church is there for. God intends to put the world to rights; he has dramatically launched this project through Jesus. Those who belong to Jesus are called, here and now, in the power of the Spirit, to be agents of that putting-to-rights purpose. The word "mission" comes from the Latin for "send": "As the father sent me," said Jesus after his resurrection, "so I am sending you" (John 20:21).

We shall consider presently what that means in practice. But first, notice this. From the very beginning, in Jesus's own teaching, it has been clear that people who are called to be agents of God's healing love, putting the world to rights, are called also to be people whose own lives are put to rights by the same healing love. The messengers must model the message. That's why, though the reason for God's call of the church is mission, the missionaries—that is, all Christians—are themselves defined as people who have themselves been made whole. We must now pause and ask what exactly that means.

Waking Up to the Good News

What happens when you wake up in the morning?

For some people, waking up is a rude and shocking experience. Off goes the alarm, and they jump in fright, dragged out of a deep sleep to face the cold, cruel light of day.

For others, it's a quiet, slow process. They can be half-asleep and half-awake, not even sure which is which, until gradually, eventually, without any shock or resentment, they are happy to know that another day has begun.

Most of us know something of both, and a lot in between.

Waking up offers one of the most basic pictures of what can happen when God takes a hand in someone's life.

There are classic alarm-clock stories. Saul of Tarsus on the road to Damascus, blinded by a sudden light, stunned and speechless, discovered that the God he had worshipped had revealed himself in the crucified and risen Jesus of Nazareth. John Wesley found his heart becoming strangely warm, and he never looked back. They and a few others are the famous ones, but there are millions more.

And there are many stories, though they don't hit the headlines in the same way, of the half-awake and half-asleep variety. Some people take months, years, maybe even decades, during which they aren't sure whether they're on the outside of Christian faith looking in, or on the inside looking around to see if it's real.

As with ordinary waking up, there are many people who are somewhere in between. But the point is that there's such a thing as being asleep, and there's such a thing as being awake. And it's important to tell the difference, and to be sure you're awake by the time you have to be up and ready for action, whatever that action may be.

Waking up is, in fact, one of the regular early Christian images for what happens when the gospel of Jesus—the good news that the creator God has acted decisively to put the world to rights— impinges on someone's consciousness. There's a good reason for this. "Sleep" was a regular way of talking about death in the ancient Jewish world. With the resurrection of Jesus, the world was being invited to wake up. "Wake up, sleeper!" writes St. Paul. "Rise from the dead! Christ will give you light!" (Ephesians 5:14).

The earliest Christians believed, in fact, that resurrection was what every human being really needed—not just in the end, in the new world that God will eventually make, but in the present life as well. God intends, in the end, to give us a new life, in comparison with which the present one is a mere thing of shadows. He intends to give us new life within his ultimate new creation. *But the new creation has already begun with the resurrection of Jesus,* and God wants us to wake up *now,* in the present time, to the new reality. We are to come through death and out the other side into a new sort of life; to become daytime people, even though the rest of the world isn't yet awake. We are to live in the present darkness by the light of Christ, so that when the sun comes up at last we will be ready for it. Or, to change the image, we are already to be penciling the sketches for the masterpiece that God will one day call us to help him paint. That's what it means to respond to the call of the Christian gospel.

It isn't, in other words, a matter of "having a new religious experience." It may feel like that, or it may not. For some people, becoming a Christian is a deeply emotional experience; for others, it's a calm, clear-eyed resolution of matters long pondered. Our personalities are gloriously different, and God treats us all gloriously differently. In any case, some religious experiences are profoundly un- or anti-Christian. The ancient world was full of all kinds of religions, many of them deeply dehumanizing. Though we don't always recognize it, the modern world is like that, too.

So what is involved in hearing and responding to the Christian gospel? What does it mean to wake up to God's new world? What does it mean, in other words, to become a member of God's people, of Jesus's people—of the church?

The gospel—the "good news" of what the creator God has done in Jesus—is first and foremost *news about something that has happened.* And the first and most appropriate response to that news is *to believe it.* God has raised Jesus from the dead, and has thereby declared in a single powerful action that Jesus has launched the long-awaited kingdom of God, and that (by means of Jesus's death) the evil of all the world has been defeated at last. When the alarm clock goes off, this is what it says: "Here's the good news. Wake up and believe it!"

This message, though, is so utterly unlikely and extraordinary that you can't expect people simply to believe it in the same way they might believe you if you said it was raining outside. And yet, as people hear the message, at least some find that they *do* believe it. It makes sense to them. I don't mean the kind of "sense" you get within the flatland world of secular imagination. There the only things that matter are what you can put into a test tube or a bank account. I mean the kind of sense that exists within the strange new world which we glimpse, even if only for a moment, in the way we glimpse a whole new world when we stand in awe in front of a great painting, or are swept off our feet by a song or a symphony. That kind of "making sense" is much more like falling in love than like calculating a bank balance. Ultimately, believing *that* God raised Jesus from the dead is a matter of believing and trusting *in* the God who would, and did, do such a thing.

This is where our word "belief" can be inadequate or even misleading. What the early Christians meant by "belief" included both believing *that* God had done certain things and believing *in* the God who had done them. This is not belief that God exists, though clearly that is involved, too, but loving, grateful trust.

When things "make sense" in that way, you are left knowing that it isn't so much a matter of you figuring it all out and deciding to take a step, or a stand. It's a matter of Someone calling you, calling with a voice you dimly recognize, calling with a message that is simultaneously an invitation of love and a summons to obedience. The call to faith is both of these. It is the call to believe that the true God, the world's creator, has loved the whole world so much, you and me included, that he has come himself in the person of his Son and has died and risen again to exhaust the power of evil and create a new world in which everything will be put to rights and joy will replace sorrow.

The more conscious we are of our own inability to get it right, perhaps even our own flagrant disloyalty to the call to live as genuine human beings, the more we will hear this call as what it most

deeply is. It is the offer of *forgiveness*. It is the summons to receive
God's gift of a slate wiped clean, a totally new start. Even to glimpse
that is to catch your breath with awe and gratitude, and to find an
answering, thankful love welling up inside. As we saw earlier, just
as you can't set up a staircase of human logic and climb up it to
get to some kind of "proof" of God, so you can't set up a staircase
of human moral or cultural achievement and climb up it to earn
God's favor. From time to time some Christians have imagined
that they were supposed to do just that, and in their efforts they've
made a nonsense of everything.

But the fact that we can't ever earn God's favor by our own
moral effort shouldn't blind us to the fact that the call to faith
is also a call to obedience. It must be, because it declares that
Jesus is the world's rightful Lord and Master. (The language Paul
used of Jesus would have reminded his hearers at once of the
language they were accustomed to hearing about Caesar.) That's
why Paul can speak about "the obedience of faith." Indeed, the
word the early Christians used for "faith" can also mean "loyalty" or "allegiance." It's what emperors ancient and modern have
always demanded of their subjects. The message of the gospel is
the good news that Jesus is the one true "emperor," ruling the
world with his own brand of self-giving love. This, of course,
cheerfully and deliberately deconstructs the word "emperor" itself.
When the early Christians used "imperial" language in relation
to Jesus, they were always conscious of irony. Whoever heard of a
crucified emperor?

When we see ourselves in the light of Jesus's type of kingdom,
and realize the extent to which we have been living by a different code altogether, we realize, perhaps for the first time, how far
we have fallen short of what we were made to be. This realization
is what we call "repentance," a serious turning away from patterns
of life which deface and distort our genuine humanness. It isn't
just a matter of feeling sorry for particular failings, though that will
often be true as well. It is the recognition that the living God has

made us humans to reflect his image into his world, and that we haven't done so. (The technical term for that is "sin," whose primary meaning is not "breaking the rules" but "missing the mark," failing to hit the target of complete, genuine, glorious humanness.) Once again, the gospel itself, the very message which announces that Jesus is Lord and calls us to obedience, contains the remedy: forgiveness, unearned and freely given, because of his cross. All we can say is, "Thank you."

To believe, to love, to obey (and to repent of our failure to do those things): faith of this kind is the mark of the Christian, the one and only badge we wear. That is why, in most traditional churches, the community declares its faith publicly in the words of one of the ancient creeds. This is the stamp of who we are. When we declare our faith, we are saying yes to this God, and to this project. That is the central mark of our identity, of who and what the church is. This, by the way, is what St. Paul meant when he spoke of "justification by faith." God declares that those who share this faith are "in the right." He intends to put the whole world to rights; he has already begun this process in the death and resurrection of Jesus, and in the work of his Spirit in the lives of men and women, bringing them to the faith by which alone we are identified as belonging to Jesus. When people come to Christian faith, they are "put in the right" as an advance sign, and as part of the means, of what God intends to do for his whole creation.

Christian faith isn't a general religious awareness. Nor is it the ability to believe several unlikely propositions. It is certainly not a kind of gullibility which would put us out of touch with any genuine reality. It is the faith which hears the story of Jesus, including the announcement that he is the world's true Lord, and responds from the heart with a surge of grateful love that says: "Yes. Jesus is Lord. He died for my sins. God raised him from the dead. This is the center of everything." Whether you come to this faith in a blinding flash or by a long, slow, winding route, once you get to this point you are (whether you realize it or not) wearing the badge which marks you out as part of the church, on an equal footing with every other Christian who ever lived. You are discovering what it means to wake up and find yourself in God's new world.

What's more, you are giving clear evidence that a new life has begun. Somewhere in the depths of your being something has stirred into life that was previously not there. It is because of this that many early Christians reached for the language of *birth*. Jesus himself, in a famous discussion with a Jewish teacher, spoke of being born "from above": a new event similar to, though distinguished from, ordinary human birth (John 3). Many early Christians picked up and developed this idea. As a newborn baby breathes and cries, so the signs of life in a newborn Christian are faith and repentance, inhaling the love of God and exhaling an initial cry of distress. And at that point what God provides, exactly as for a newborn infant, is the comfort, protection, and nurturing promise of a mother.

Belonging to the Family

"If God is our father, the church is our mother." The words are those of the Swiss Reformer John Calvin. Several biblical passages speak in this way (notably, Galatians 4:26–27, echoing Isaiah 54:1). They underline the fact that it is as impossible, unnecessary, and undesirable to be a Christian all by yourself as it is to be a newborn baby all by yourself.

The church is first and foremost a *community*, a collection of people who belong to one another because they belong to God, the God we know in and through Jesus. Though we often use the word "church" to denote a building, the point is that it's the building *where this community meets*. True, buildings can and do carry memories, and when people have been praying and worshipping and mourning and celebrating in a particular building for many years, the building itself may come to speak powerfully of God's welcoming presence. But it is the *people* who matter.

The church exists primarily for two closely correlated purposes: to worship God and to work for his kingdom in the world. You can and must worship, and work for God's kingdom, in private and in ways unique to yourself, but if God's kingdom is to go forward, rather than around and around in circles, we must work together as well as apart.

The church also exists for a third purpose, which serves the other two: to encourage one another, to build one another up in faith, to pray with and for one another, to learn from one another and teach one another, and to set one another examples to follow, challenges to take up, and urgent tasks to perform. This is all part of what is known loosely as *fellowship*. This doesn't just mean serving one another cups of tea and coffee. It's all about living within that sense of a joint enterprise, a family business, in which everyone has a proper share and a proper place.

It is within this context that the different "ministries" within the church have grown up. From the very earliest evidence we have, in the Acts of the Apostles and the letters of Paul, the church has recognized different callings within its common life. God has given different gifts to different people so that the whole community may flourish and take forward the work with which it has been entrusted.

Worship, fellowship, and the work of reflecting God's kingdom into the world flow into and out of one another. You can't reflect God's image without returning to worship to keep the reflection fresh and authentic. In the same way, worship sustains and nourishes fellowship; without it, fellowship quickly deteriorates into groups of the like-minded, which in turn quickly become exclusive cliques—the very opposite of what Jesus's people should be aiming at.

It is within the church, even when the church isn't getting everything quite right, that the Christian faith of which we have spoken is nourished and grows to maturity. As with any family, the members discover who they are in relationship with one another. Churches vary enormously in size, from scattered handfuls of people in isolated villages to enormous congregations of many thousands in some parts of the world. But ideally every Christian should belong to a group that is small enough for individuals to get to know and care for each other, and particularly to pray in meaningful depth for one another, and also to a fellowship large enough to contain a wide variety in its membership, styles of worship, and kingdom-activity. The smaller the local community, the more important it is to be powerfully linked to a larger unit. The larger the regular gathering (I think of those churches where several hundred, or even several thousand, meet together every week), the more important it is for each member to belong also to a smaller group. Ideally, groups of a dozen or so will meet to pray, study scripture, and build one another up in the faith.

Membership of the church begins with a single action which speaks dramatically of what believing and belonging is all about: baptism.

Through the Waters of Baptism

We ought to know the story by now. Jews, ancient and modern, have told it every year and in graphic detail: the story of how God rescued them from Egypt. He brought them through the Red Sea and led them through the wilderness into the Promised Land. *Through the water to freedom.*

The story itself began, interestingly, with the leader, Moses, being rescued as a little boy from the reedy edge of the Nile River, after his parents had placed him there in a waterproof basket rather than kill him as they had been ordered to do. Moses had to go through (on a small scale) the rescue-through-water which God would accomplish through him later on. After Moses's death, it happened again: Joshua led the people through the Jordan River and into the Promised Land at last.

These stories look back even further. Creation itself took place, according to Genesis 1, when God's great wind or breath or Spirit brooded like a dove over the waters, and when God separated the waters into different places and called dry land to appear. Creation itself, you might say, began with an exodus, a baptism. *Through the water to new life.*

So we shouldn't be surprised when we find that one of the best-known Jewish renewal movements took shape as a new-exodus movement, and a crossing-the-Jordan movement. Jesus's cousin John believed it was his calling to get people ready for the long-awaited moment when Israel's God would fulfill his ancient promises. He called people out into the Judaean wilderness to be baptized (the word means literally "plunged") into the Jordan River, confessing their sins. *Through the water into God's new covenant.* They were to be the purified people, the new-covenant people, the people ready for their God to come and deliver them.

Jesus himself submitted to John's baptism. He was identifying with those he had come to rescue, fulfilling the covenant plan of his Father. And as he came up from the water, God's Spirit descended on him like a dove, with a voice from heaven declaring that he was God's true Son, Israel's Messiah, the king. Jesus saw his kingdom-movement as starting with that symbolic new-exodus action.

But he also saw it pointing to the action with which his ministry would reach its climax. He spoke on one occasion about having "a baptism to be baptized with"—and it became clear that he was referring to his own death. As we saw earlier, he chose Passover, the great Jewish exodus festival, as the moment to act symbolically to challenge the authorities, knowing what was bound to happen next.

Jesus's own baptism and his carefully planned Last Supper both point back to the original exodus (the coming-through-the-water moment), point behind that to the original creation itself, and finally point on to Jesus's death and resurrection as the new defining reality, the moment of new covenant, new creation. And to achieve that renewal it was necessary to go, not just through the water and out the other side, but through a deeper flood altogether. All the multiple layers of meaning that were already present in baptism were now to be recentered on the event of Jesus's death and resurrection. *Through the water into God's new world.*

That is why, from the earliest Christian sources we possess, Christian baptism is linked not just to Jesus's own baptism, not just to the exodus and the first creation, but to Jesus's death and resurrection. St. Paul, in one of his earliest letters, speaks of being "crucified with the Messiah" and coming through into a new life; and in his greatest work (the letter to Rome) he explains that in baptism itself we die "with the Messiah" and come through to share his risen life. The spectacular, unique events at the heart of the Christian story *happen to us,* not just at the end of our own lives and beyond (when we die physically and, eventually, when we rise again), but while we are continuing to live in the present time. *Through the water into the new life of belonging to Jesus.*

That is why, from very early on, Christian baptism was seen as the mode of entry into the Christian family, and why it was associated with the idea of being "born again." Of course, not everyone who has been through water-baptism has actually known and experienced for themselves the saving love of God in Christ sweeping through and transforming their lives. At various points Paul has to remind his readers that they have a responsibility to make real in their own lives the truth of what happened to them in baptism. But he doesn't say that baptism doesn't matter, or that it isn't real. People who have been baptized can choose to reject the faith, just as the children of Israel could rebel against YHWH after having come through the Red Sea. Paul makes that point in 1 Corinthians 10 and elsewhere. But they can't get unbaptized: God will regard them as disobedient family members rather than outsiders.

In particular, we can now see why Christian baptism involves being plunged into water (or having it poured over you) in the name of God, Father, Son, and Holy Spirit. The point is that the story which baptism tells is God's own story, from creation and covenant to new covenant and new creation, with Jesus in the middle of it and the Spirit brooding over it. In baptism, *you* are brought into that story, to be an actor in the play which God is writing and producing. And once you're onstage, you're part of the action. You can get the lines wrong. You can do your best to spoil the play. But the story is moving forward, and it would be far better to understand where it's going and how to learn your lines and join in the drama. *Through the water to become part of God's purpose for the world.*

†

Sixteen

New Creation, Starting Now

Despite what many people think, within the Christian family and outside it, the point of Christianity isn't "to go to heaven when you die."

The New Testament picks up from the Old the theme that God intends, in the end, to put the whole creation to rights. Earth and heaven were made to overlap with one another, not fitfully, mysteriously, and partially as they do at the moment, but completely, gloriously, and utterly. "The earth shall be filled with the glory of God as the waters cover the sea." That is the promise which resonates throughout the Bible story, from Isaiah (and behind him, by implication, from Genesis itself) all the way through to Paul's greatest visionary moments and the final chapters of the book of Revelation. The great drama will end, not with "saved souls" being snatched up into heaven, away from the wicked earth and the mortal bodies which have dragged them down into sin, but with the New Jerusalem coming down from heaven to earth, so that "the dwelling of God is with humans" (Revelation 21:3).

A little over a hundred years ago, an American pastor in upstate New York celebrated in a great hymn both the beauty of creation and the presence of the creator God within it. His name was Maltbie Babcock, and his hymn "This Is My Father's World" points beyond the present beauty of creation, through the mess and tragedy with which it has been infected, to the ultimate resolution. There are different versions of the relevant stanza, but this one is the clearest:

> *This is my Father's world; O let me ne'er forget*
> *That though the wrong seems oft so strong,*
> *God is the ruler yet.*
> *This is my Father's world; the battle is not done;*
> *Jesus, who died, shall be satisfied,*
> *And earth and heaven be one.*

And earth and heaven be one: that is the note that should sound like a clear, sweet bell through all Christian living, summoning us to live in the present as people called to that future, people called to live in the present in the light of that future. The two themes to which we have returned again and again in this book—the overlap of heaven and earth and the overlap of God's future with our present time—come together once more as we look at what it means for believing and baptized members of God's people to live under the lordship of Jesus within the present world. And as we look at these themes, of the launching of new creation in the present, we discover at last that we are called not only to listen to the echoes of the voice we heard in the early part of this book, but to be people through whom the rest of the world comes to hear and respond to that voice as well.

Paul and John, Jesus himself, and pretty well all the great Christian teachers of the first two centuries stressed their belief in *resurrection.* "Resurrection" doesn't mean "going to heaven when you die." It isn't about "life after death." As we saw in Chapter Eight, it's about "life *after* 'life after death.'" After you die, you go to be "with Christ" ("life after death"), but your body remains dead. Describing where and what you are in that interim period is difficult, and for the most part the New Testament writers don't try. Call it "heaven" if you like, but don't imagine that it's the end of all things. What is promised *after* that interim period is a new bodily life within God's new world ("life *after* 'life after death'").

I am constantly amazed that many contemporary Christians find this confusing. It was second nature to the early church and to many subsequent Christian generations. It was what they believed and taught. If we have grown up believing and teaching something else, it's time we rubbed our eyes and read our texts again. God's plan is not to abandon this world, the world which he said was "very good." Rather, he intends to remake it. And when he does, he will raise all his people to new *bodily* life to live in it. That is the promise of the Christian gospel.

To live in it, yes; and also to rule over it. There is a mystery here which few today have even begun to ponder. Both Paul and Revelation stress that in God's new world those who belong to the Messiah will be placed in charge. The first creation was put into the care of God's image-bearing creatures. The new creation will be put into the wise, healing stewardship of those who have been "renewed according to the image of the creator," as Paul puts it (Colossians 3:10).

In God's new world Jesus himself will of course be the central figure. That's why from the very beginning the church has always spoken of his "second coming," though in terms of the overlap of heaven and earth it would be more appropriate to speak, as some early Christians also did, of the "reappearing" of Jesus. He is, at the moment, present with us, but hidden behind that invisible veil which keeps heaven and earth apart, and which we pierce in those moments, such as prayer, the sacraments, the reading of scripture, and our work with the poor, when the veil seems particularly thin. But one day the veil will be lifted; earth and heaven will be one; Jesus will be personally present, and every knee shall bow at his name; creation will be renewed; the dead will be raised; and God's new world will at last be in place, full of new prospects and possibilities. This is what the Christian vision of salvation—a word I haven't used until now, because it's often misunderstood—is all about.

But if that is where we're going, what road must we take to get there?

Living Between Heaven and Earth

Our vision of the road from here to there, from creation to new creation—in other words, the way we are called to live in the present—will vary not just according to what we conceive to be the final destination, but also according to the whole way we understand God and the world.

We need to revisit one last time the three options we set out earlier for understanding how God and the world are related. Option One was to see God and the world as basically the same thing, already overlapping more or less entirely. The pantheist, and to a lesser extent the panentheist, seeks to get in touch or in tune with the divine impulses present within the world and within oneself. As we saw, it's difficult within such a scheme to have much sense of anything being radically evil. Many pantheists are deeply moral people who have struggled to express what it means for human beings to live in accordance with the true divinity within the created order. But this option isn't the way to a fully Christian morality or ethic.

Option Two was to see God and the world as a long way apart from one another. Many today, faced with the question of Christian ethics, assume this model, taking it for granted that if this distant God wanted humans to behave in particular ways he would give them instructions. The idea of an overarching moral law, common to all humankind, written perhaps within human consciences but also needing to be thought out, argued through, and taught, has been extremely common in Western society for the last two hundred years at least. Indeed, many people have supposed that when St. Paul was talking about "the law," he was referring to that sort of overarching moral system. Christian ethics then becomes a matter of struggling to obey a somewhat arbitrary code of law promulgated by a distant deity. Within that struggle, "sin" is seen in terms of breaking laws conceived in that fashion; and "salvation" is the rescue of human beings from the punishment that this deity would otherwise inflict on those who disobey his decrees. Again, though this has some echoes of Christianity, it isn't in fact the Christian way.

Options One and Two reinforce each other by reaction. The pantheist or panentheist looks at Option Two and shudders at the thought of that remote, detached deity, his arbitrary laws, and his haughty and apparently malevolent attitude toward the human race. The Deist looks at Option One and shudders at the thought of the semi-paganism involved in simply trying to get in touch with forces and impulses within the world the way it is. This game is played out on a thousand fields in contemporary discussions of everything from politics to sex to the meaning of the cross. And it misses the point.

According to Option Three, God and the world are different from one another, but not far apart. There were and are ways in which, moments at which, and events through which heaven and earth overlap and interlock. For the devout first-century Jew, the Torah wasn't the arbitrary decree of a distant deity, but the covenant charter which bound Israel to YHWH. It was the pathway along which one might discover what genuine humanness was all about. If all Israel managed to keep the Torah for a single day, declared some Jewish teachers, the Age to Come would have begun. The Torah was the road into God's future. Of course it was; because, like the Temple, it was a place where heaven and earth overlapped, where you might glimpse what it would be like when they became completely one. The same was true of Wisdom, the blueprint for creation and also the blueprint for genuine human living.

Yes, replied the early Christians: and Temple, Torah, and Wisdom have come together in and as Jesus of Nazareth, Israel's Messiah, God's second self, his "Son" in that full sense. And, with that, God's future has arrived in the present, has arrived in the person of Jesus. In arriving, it has confronted and defeated the forces of evil and opened the way for God's new world, for heaven and earth to be joined forever. In the Christian version of Option Three, not only heaven and earth, but also future and present, overlap and interlock. And the way that interlocking becomes real, not just imaginary, is through the powerful work of God's Spirit.

This is the launchpad for the specifically Christian way of life. That way of life isn't a matter simply of getting in touch with our inner depths. It is certainly not about keeping the commands of a distant deity. Rather, it is the new way of being human, the Jesus-shaped way of being human, the cross-and-resurrection way of life, the Spirit-led pathway. It is the way which anticipates, in the present, the full, rich, glad human existence which will one day be ours when God makes all things new. Christian ethics is not a matter of discovering what's going on in the world and getting in tune with it. It isn't a matter of doing things to earn God's favor. It is not about trying to obey dusty rulebooks from long ago or far away. It is about practicing, in the present, the tunes we shall sing in God's new world.

Renounce and Rediscover

Once we get that clear, the way is open to a fresh account of what it means to live as a Christian—and, within that, to demonstrate at least in outline the ways in which Christian living responds to the echoes we heard in Part One of this book.

Christian living means dying with Christ and rising again. That, as we saw, is part of the meaning of baptism, the starting point of the Christian pilgrimage. The model of pilgrimage is helpful, since baptism awakens echoes of the children of Israel coming out of Egypt and going off to the Promised Land. The whole world is now God's holy land, and God will reclaim it and renew it as the ultimate goal of all our wanderings.

We begin our pilgrimage with the death and resurrection of Jesus. Our goal is the renewal of the presently corrupt creation. This makes it clear that the route through the wilderness, the path of our pilgrimage, will involve two things in particular: renunciation on the one hand and rediscovery on the other.

Renunciation. The world in its present state is out of tune with God's ultimate intention, and there will be a great many things, some of them deeply woven into our imagination and personality, to which the only Christian response will be "no." Jesus told his followers that if they wanted to come after him they would have to deny themselves and take up their cross. The only way to find yourself, he said, is to lose yourself (a strikingly different agenda from today's finding-out-who-I-really-am philosophies). From the very beginning, writers like Paul and John recognized that this isn't just difficult, but actually impossible. We can't do it by some kind of Herculean moral effort. The only way is by drawing strength from beyond ourselves, the strength of God's Spirit, on the basis of our sharing of Jesus's death and resurrection in baptism.

Rediscovery. New creation is not a denial of our humanness, but its reaffirmation; and there will be a great many things, some of them deeply counterintuitive and initially perplexing, to which the proper Christian response is "yes." The resurrection of Jesus enables us to see how it is that living as a Christian isn't simply a matter of discovering the inner truth of the way the world currently is, or simply a matter of learning a way of life that is in tune with a different world and thus completely out of tune with the present one. It is a matter of glimpsing that in God's new creation, of which Jesus's resurrection is the start, all that was good in the original creation is reaffirmed. All that has corrupted and defaced it—including many things which are woven so tightly into the fabric of the world as we know it that we can't imagine being without them—will be done away. Learning to live as a Christian is learning to live as a renewed human being, anticipating the eventual new creation in and with a world which is still longing and groaning for that final redemption.

The problem is that it is by no means clear what to renounce and what to rediscover. How can we say no to things which seem so much a part of life that to reject them appears to us to be the rejection of part of God's good creation? How can we say yes to things which many Christians have seen not as good and right but as dangerous and deluded? How can we (the same old question once more) avoid dualism on the one hand and paganism on the other? Somehow we have to work out which styles of life and behavior belong with the corrupting evil which must be rejected if new creation is to emerge, and which styles of life and behavior belong with the new creation which must be embraced, struggled for, and celebrated.

This takes nerves of steel, and a careful searching after wisdom. We are to be informed by the life, teaching, death, and resurrection of Jesus; by the leading of the Spirit; by the wisdom we find in scripture; by the fact of our baptism and all that it means; by the sense of God's presence and guidance through prayer; and by the fellowship of other Christians, both our contemporaries and those of other ages whose lives and writings are ours to use as wise guides. Listing all these in that fashion makes them sound as if they are separate sources of teaching, but in reality it isn't like that. They work together in a hundred different ways. Part of the art of being a Christian is learning to be sensitive to all of them, and to weigh what we think we are hearing from one quarter alongside what is being said in another.

Only when we have set all that out quite clearly can we ever speak of "rules." There *are* rules, of course. The New Testament has plenty of them. Always give alms in secret. Never sue a fellow Christian. Never take private vengeance. Be kind. Always show hospitality. Give away money cheerfully. Don't be anxious. Don't judge another Christian over a matter of conscience. Always forgive. And so on. And the worrying thing about that randomly selected list is that most Christians ignore most of them most of the time. It isn't so much that we lack clear rules; we lack, I fear, the teaching that will draw attention to what is in fact there in our primary documents, not least in the teaching of Jesus himself.

The rules are to be understood, not as arbitrary laws thought up by a distant God to stop us from having fun (or to set us some ethical hoops to jump through as a kind of moral examination), but as the signposts to a way of life in which heaven and earth overlap, in which God's future breaks into the present, in which we discover what genuine humanness looks and feels like in practice.

When we start to glimpse that, we discover that the echoes we heard at the start of this book have indeed turned into a voice. It is, of course, the voice of Jesus, calling us to follow him into God's new world—the world in which the hints, signposts, and echoes of the present world turn into the reality of the next one. We've already considered, at some length, the spirituality which the Christian gospel is meant to generate and sustain. We turn, in conclusion, to the other three "echoes": justice, relationships, and beauty.

Justice Revisited

God does indeed intend to put the world to rights. There is a cry for justice which wells up from our hearts, not only when we are wronged but when we see others being wronged. It is a response to the longing, and the demand, of the living God that his world should be a place not of moral anarchy, where the bullies always win in the end, but of fair and straight dealings, of honesty, truthfulness, and uprightness.

But to get from that longing and demand to anything that approaches God's intended justice, we must go by a route very different from the one which the world normally expects and even demands. The majority language of the world in this respect is violence. When people with power see things happen of which they disapprove, they drop bombs and send in tanks. When people without power see things happen of which they disapprove, they smash store windows, blow themselves up in crowded places, and fly planes into buildings. The fact that both methods have proved remarkably unsuccessful at changing things doesn't stop people from going on in the same way.

On the cross the living God took the fury and violence of the world onto himself, suffering massive injustice—the biblical stories are careful to highlight this—and yet refusing to lash out with threats or curses. Part of what Christians have called "atonement theology" is the belief that in some sense or other Jesus exhausted the underlying power of evil when he died under its weight, refusing to pass it on or keep it in circulation. Jesus's resurrection is the beginning of a world in which a new type of justice is possible. Through the hard work of prayer, persuasion, and political action, it is possible to make governments on the one hand and revolutionary groups on the other see that there is a different approach than unremitting violence, than fighting force with force. The (mostly) quiet, prayerful revolutions that overturned eastern European Communism are a wonderful example. The extraordinary work of Desmond Tutu in South Africa is another. The attempts to initiate programs of "restorative justice" within police work and criminal justice systems offer yet another. In each case, onlookers have been tempted to suggest that the way of nonviolence appears weak and ineffectual. The results suggest otherwise.

To work for a healing, restorative justice—whether in individual relationships, in international relations, or anywhere in between—is therefore a primary Christian calling. It determines one whole sphere of Christian behavior. Violence and personal vengeance are ruled out, as the New Testament makes abundantly clear. Every Christian is called to work, at every level of life, for a world in which reconciliation and restoration are put into practice, and so to anticipate that day when God will indeed put everything to rights.

This does *not* mean advocating a holy anarchy in which there is no order, no government, no means of enforcing laws, within society as a whole. Interestingly, the very passage in which Paul forbids private vengeance (the end of Romans 12) is followed at once by the passage in which he most clearly says that God intends societies to be well ordered and firmly governed (the start of Romans 13). God, as the wise creator, uses authorities, even where they do not acknowledge him and even when they make many mistakes, to bring at least a measure of order into his world. The alternative is the breakdown of social and cultural order, a situation in which the powerful and wealthy always win. Precisely because God cares passionately about the weak and the poor, he intends that there should be governments and authorities who can keep in check those who through greed and force would otherwise exploit them. God would no doubt prefer it if the ruling authorities did in fact acknowledge him and try to bring their laws more directly into line with his will. Indeed, Christians should campaign for this— for instance, in matters such as global debt—on the grounds that it is good for all, not simply that it is what our tradition proposes. Yet even where the authorities do not acknowledge God, he uses them, in some measure at least, to restrain evil and encourage virtue. Finding out what this will mean in the international community of today's global village, as well as within individual countries, is one of the major questions we face today.

Nor does working for reconciliation and restorative justice mean ignoring the fact that there is such a thing as evil. Indeed, it demands that we take evil actions very seriously indeed. Only when they have been named, acknowledged, and dealt with can reconciliation take place. Otherwise all we have is a parody of the gospel, a kind of cheap grace in which everybody pretends that everything is all right while knowing perfectly well that it isn't. Discovering how to address evil both locally and globally is another of the major tasks facing us today. The Christian gospel challenges us to grow up morally in ways never dreamed of by much of the world.

The cry for justice in the world, then, must be taken up and amplified by the Christian church, as the proper response to the voice of the living God. The gospel of Jesus Christ and the power of the Spirit indicate that there are ways forward. This calling can and should generate programs and agendas in several different areas, from globalization and fair trade to governmental and societal reform, from highlighting the plight of disadvantaged minorities to spotlighting the actions of powerful governments in squelching opposition both at home and abroad. Christians should be energetic in advocating and pursuing that justice for which all human beings long and which burst upon the world, in a fresh and unexpected way, through Jesus.

Relationships Rediscovered

Relationships remain central to all human life. Even hermits need someone to bring them food and water, and many solitary souls choose, as part of their daily task, to pray for people near and far. Justice speaks of the ordering of our relationships at all levels, not least on the larger scale of society and the world as a whole; but the longing for relationship goes much deeper than merely avoiding unfairness and getting one's rights. It speaks of intimacy, friendship, mutual delight, admiration, and respect. It speaks of that which, for many people much of the time, makes life worth living. Again and again in the New Testament it is clear that the Christian community is called upon to model new patterns of human relating, new standards for how to treat one another.

The key word, of course, is "love," and much has been written about that in itself. But I want to draw attention to something else—something often ignored in the clamor for better and clearer rules of Christian behavior: that we should be positively kind to one another. "Be kind to one another, tender-hearted, forgiving one another, as God in Christ has forgiven you. Therefore be imitators of God, as beloved children, and live in love, as Christ loved us and gave himself up for us" (Ephesians 4:32–5:2). The quest for justice all too easily degenerates into the demand for *my* rights or *our* rights. The command of kindness asks that we spend our time looking not at ourselves and our needs, our rights, our wrongs-that-need-righting, but at everyone else and their needs, pressures, pains, and joys. Kindness is a primary way of growing up as a human being, of establishing and maintaining the richest and deepest relationships.

That is why Christians are called to learn how to cope with anger. It will happen; being angry is inevitable as part of the brokenness of the world. We would have to develop the hide of a rhinoceros not to become angry from time to time. But the question is, What will we do with our anger? Here again Paul's command is clear, brisk, and practical. Be angry but don't sin (he is probably alluding to Psalm 4:4). Don't let sunset find you still angry. Keep short accounts—in other words, don't let things fester and get worse. No bitterness; no wrath, anger, slander, malice, or abuse. No lying either (Ephesians 4:25–31; Colossians 3:8–9). It is worth pondering the patterns of relationships we know about, and asking ourselves how different they would be if everyone involved were, even if only in principle, signed up to live according to these precepts. And if such a life seems impossible, the answer is that forgiveness is always to be the order of the day. That is what we should expect for a people who pray the Lord's Prayer.

Once again we see, under the heading of what we might call "ethics," the victory of the cross of Jesus Christ and the power of the Spirit. The New Testament's appeal for a new way of relating to one another—a way of kindness, a way which accepts the fact of anger but refuses to allow it to dictate the terms of engagement—is based foursquare on the achievement of Jesus. His death has accomplished our forgiveness; very well, we must then pass that on to one another. We must become, must be known as, the people who don't hold grudges, who don't sulk. We must be the people who know how to say "Sorry," and who know how to respond when other people say it to us. It is remarkable, once more, how difficult this still seems, considering how much time the Christian church has had to think about it and how much energy has been spent on expounding the New Testament, where the advice is all so clear. Perhaps it's because we have tried, if at all, to do it as though it were

just a matter of obeying an artificial command—and then, finding
it difficult, have stopped trying because nobody else seems to be
very good at it either. Perhaps it might be different if we reminded ourselves frequently that we are preparing for life in God's new
world, and that the death and resurrection of Jesus, which by baptism constitute our own new identity, offer us both the motivation
and the energy to try again in a new way.

Near the center of any discussion of relationships we find, naturally, the question of sex. Here again the New Testament is stark and
brisk. As in its discussion of anger, it uses plenty of different terms,
as though to make sure that none of the distortions of human sexu-
ality (which were as well known in the ancient world as they are in
our own day) would be able to slip through by default. Sample the
wares at any newsstand in the Western world; watch television for
a day or two; stroll through the cities where so many people con-
gregate—and then ponder passages like these:

> Don't you know that the unjust won't inherit God's king-
> dom? Don't be deceived! Neither immoral people, nor
> idolaters, nor adulterers, nor practicing homosexuals of
> whichever sort, nor thieves, nor greedy people, nor drunk-
> ards, nor abusive talkers, nor robbers will inherit God's king-
> dom. That, of course, is what some of you were! But you
> were washed clean; you were made holy; you were put back
> to rights—in the name of the Lord, King Jesus, and in the
> Spirit of our God.
>
> (1 Corinthians 6:9–11)

> As for fornication, uncleanness of any kind, or greed: you
> shouldn't even mention them! You are, after all, God's holy
> people. Shameful, stupid, or coarse conversation is quite out
> of place. Instead, there should be thanksgiving.
>
> You should know this, you see: no fornicator, nobody who
> practices uncleanness, no greedy person (in other words, an

idolater), has any inheritance in the Messiah's kingdom, or in God's. Don't let anyone fool you with empty words. It's because of these things, you see, that God's wrath is coming on people who are disobedient.

So don't share in their practices. After all, at one time you were darkness, but now, in the Lord, you are light! So behave as children of light. Light has its fruit, doesn't it, in everything that's good, and just, and true. Think through what's going to be pleasing to the Lord. Work it out.

(Ephesians 5:3–10)

So, then, you must kill off the parts of you that belong on the earth: illicit sexual behavior, uncleanness, passion, evil desire, and greed (which is a form of idolatry). It's because of these things that God's wrath comes on disobedient people. You too used to behave like that, once, when your life consisted of that sort of thing. But now you must put away the whole lot of them.

(Colossians 3:5–8)

The trouble is that the modern world, like much of the ancient one, has come to regard what is sometimes called an active sex life as not only the norm but something nobody in his or her right mind does without. The only question is, What particular forms of sexual activity do you find exciting, fulfilling, or life-enhancing? The early and normative Christian tradition, in line with the great Jewish tradition (and, for that matter, the much later Muslim tradition), stands out at this point against the normal approach of paganism ancient and modern and utters a vehement no.

Jesus himself spoke sternly about the desires which well up within the human heart: fornication, theft, murder, adultery, avarice, wickedness, deceit, licentiousness, and so on (Mark 7:21–22). Sexual misdeeds are listed alongside all kinds of other equally important categories, but that's not an excuse for saying that they don't matter. Throughout the early centuries of Christianity, when every kind of sexual behavior ever known to the human race was widely practiced throughout ancient Greek and Roman society, the Christians, like the Jews, insisted that sexual activity was to be restricted to the marriage of a man and a woman. The rest of the world, then as now, thought they were mad. The difference, alas, is that today half the church seems to think so, too.

They weren't mad. The point about new creation is that it is new *creation*. And, though we are told that procreation won't be necessary in God's new world (because people won't die), the very imagery which the Bible uses to describe that new world—imagery about the marriage of the Lamb (Revelation), or about the new world being born from the womb of the old (Romans)—indicates that the male/female relationship, woven so centrally into the story of creation in Genesis 1 and 2, is not an accidental or a temporary phenomenon, but is, rather, symbolic of the fact that creation itself carries God-given life and procreative possibility within it. Even to consider the question from this angle poses a sharp contrast to the way in which, in our present culture, sexual activity has become almost completely detached from the whole business of building up communities and relationships, and has degenerated simply into a way of asserting one's right to choose one's own pleasure in one's own way. To put it starkly: instead of being a sacrament, sex has become a toy.

The argument Paul uses in 1 Corinthians is particularly instructive in view of the way we have approached the whole subject of Christian behavior. What you do with your body matters, he says, because "God raised the Lord and will also raise us by his power" (1 Corinthians 6:14). In other words, precisely because the ultimate goal is neither a disembodied heaven nor a mere rearrangement of life on the present earth, but the redemption of the whole creation, our calling is to live in our bodies *now* in a way which anticipates the life we shall live *then*. Marital fidelity echoes and anticipates God's fidelity to the whole creation. Other kinds of sexual activity symbolize and embody the distortions and corruptions of the present world.

Christian sexual ethics, in other words, isn't simply a collection of old rules which we are now free to set aside because we know better (the danger within Option Two). Nor can we appeal against the New Testament by saying that whatever desires we find inside our deepest selves must be God-given (the natural assumption within Option One). Jesus was quite clear about that. Yes, God knows our deepest desires; but the famous old prayer which (tremblingly) acknowledges that fact doesn't go on to imply that this means they are therefore to be fulfilled and carried out as they stand, but rather that they need cleansing and healing:

> Almighty God, to whom all hearts are open, all desires known, and from whom no secrets are hidden: Cleanse the thoughts of our hearts by the inspiration of your Holy Spirit, that we may perfectly love you, and worthily magnify your holy name; through Christ our Lord. Amen.

Another famous old prayer puts it even more sharply:

> Almighty God, who alone can bring order to the unruly wills and passions of sinful humanity: Give your people grace so to love what you command and to desire what you promise, that, among the many changes of this world, our hearts may surely there be fixed, where true joys are to be found; through Jesus Christ our Lord. Amen.

We have lived for too long in a world, and tragically even in a church, where this prayer has become reversed: where the wills and affections of human beings are regarded as sacrosanct as they stand, where God is required to command what we already love and to promise what we already desire. The implicit religion of many people today is simply to discover who they really are and then try

to live it out—which is, as many have discovered, a recipe for chaotic, disjointed, and dysfunctional humanness. The logic of cross
and resurrection, of the new creation which gives shape to all truly
Christian living, points in a different direction. And one of the central names for that direction is joy: the joy of relationships healed
as well as enhanced, the joy of belonging to the new creation, of
finding not what we already had but what God was longing to give
us. At the heart of the Christian ethic is humility; at the heart of its
parodies, pride. Different roads with different destinations, and the
destinations color the character of those who travel by them.

Beauty Reborn

We come back at last to beauty. The longing for beauty, and the
sense of delight and even relief we feel when we discover it, is (as
we saw earlier) tempered with several puzzles. Beauty slips through
our fingers; the daffodil wilts, the sunset disappears, human beauty
decays and dies. The closer we come to beauty, the more it baffles
us. If we simply take the world as it is, with all its drama, delicacy,
and majesty, we tend to be pulled either toward the sentimentality
of pantheism or the brutalism of a world in which only power really matters, a world from which God seems to have vanished. (That
was more or less the point of the "brutalist" school of architecture,
whose concrete monstrosities still litter some of our cities.)

The solution I proposed earlier was that the beauty we glimpse
in creation can best be understood as one part of a larger whole,
and that the larger whole is what will be accomplished when God
renews heaven and earth. One obvious symbol for this is the haunting biblical image of the tree. The tree of knowledge in the Garden
of Eden bore the forbidden fruit, offering a wisdom to be gained
without submission to the Creator. A terrible wisdom, extracting a
terrible price; and the tree of life remained out of reach to the ban-
ished human race. But then, at the climax of the epic, the woman's descendant hung on another tree, which revealed only too

clearly the long entail of evil: violence, degradation, scornful organized religion, imperial brutality, the betrayal of friends. And yet, within a very short time, the early Christians were speaking of the cross, not as the hated sign of the callous imperial overlord, but as the ultimate revelation of the love of God. And in the last scene, in the New Jerusalem where earth and heaven meet, the tree of life grows freely on the banks of the river, its leaves offering healing to the nations. That sign of redemption speaks powerfully of beauty restored, of something in the original creation that had gone wrong now being put to rights. It serves as a pointer for the direction we must now travel, a direction once more set by the cross and resurrection.

What I want to propose, as we reach the end of this book, is that the church should reawaken its hunger for beauty at every level. This is essential and urgent. It is central to Christian living that we should celebrate the goodness of creation, ponder its present brokenness, and, insofar as we can, celebrate in advance the healing of the world, the new creation itself. Art, music, literature, dance, theater, and many other expressions of human delight and wisdom, can all be explored in new ways.

The point is this. The arts are not the pretty but irrelevant bits around the border of reality. They are highways into the center of a reality which cannot be glimpsed, let alone grasped, any other way. The present world is good, but broken and in any case incomplete; art of all kinds enables us to understand that paradox in its many dimensions. But the present world is also designed for something which has not yet happened. It is like a violin waiting to be played: beautiful to look at, graceful to hold—and yet if you'd never heard one in the hands of a musician, you wouldn't believe the new dimensions of beauty yet to be revealed. Perhaps art can show something of that, can glimpse the future possibilities pregnant within the present time. It is like a chalice: again, beautiful to look at, pleasing to hold, but waiting to be filled with the wine which, itself full of sacramental possibilities, gives the chalice its fullest meaning. Perhaps art can help us to look beyond the immediate beauty with all its puzzles, and to glimpse that new creation which makes sense not only of beauty but of the world as a whole, and ourselves within it. Perhaps.

The artist can then join forces with those who work for justice and those who struggle for redemptive relationships, and together encourage and sustain those who are reaching out for a genuine, redemptive spirituality. The way to make sense of it all is to look ahead. Look to the coming time when the earth shall be filled with the knowledge and glory of the Lord as the waters cover the sea; and then live in the present in the light of that promise, sure that it will come fully true because it was already fulfilled when God did for Jesus at Easter what he is going to do for the whole of creation. Gradually we are glimpsing a truth which cannot be overemphasized: that the tasks which await us as Christians, the paths we must walk and the lessons we must learn, are part of the great vocation which reaches us in God's word—the word of the gospel, the word of Jesus and the Spirit. We are called to be *part of* God's new creation, called to be *agents of* that new creation here and now. We are called to *model and display* that new creation in symphonies and family life, in restorative justice and poetry, in holiness and service to the poor, in politics and painting.

When you see the dawn breaking, you think back to the darkness in a new way. "Sin" is not simply the breaking of a law. It is the missing of an opportunity. Having heard the echoes of a voice, we are called to come and meet the Speaker. We are invited to be transformed by the voice itself, the word of the gospel—the word which declares that evil has been judged, that the world has been put to rights, that earth and heaven are joined forever, and that new creation has begun. We are called to become people who can speak and live and paint and sing that word so that those who have heard its echoes can come and lend a hand in the larger project. That is the opportunity that stands before us, as gift and possibility. Christian holiness is not (as people often imagine) a matter of denying something good. It is about growing up and grasping something even better.

Made for spirituality, we wallow in introspection. Made for joy, we settle for pleasure. Made for justice, we clamor for vengeance. Made for relationship, we insist on our own way. Made for beauty, we are satisfied with sentiment. But new creation has already begun. The sun has begun to rise. Christians are called to leave behind, in the tomb of Jesus Christ, all that belongs to the brokenness and incompleteness of the present world. It is time, in the power of the Spirit, to take up our proper role, our fully human role, as agents, heralds, and stewards of the new day that is dawning. That, quite simply, is what it means to be Christian: to follow Jesus Christ into the new world, God's new world, which he has thrown open before us.

Afterword

✝

To Take Things
Further ...

This book has only been able to scratch the surface of a large number of exciting and intricate topics. For those who want to take things further, to follow up brief discussions and explore things more fully for themselves, there is a wide world of literature available at every level from beginner to scholar. One of the first essentials is a good modern translation of the Bible. Actually, having two different versions is even better, since no translation is perfect and it's good to read different versions from time to time. The New Revised Standard Version is usually very reliable and readable; the New American Standard Version is widely used. The New International Version is popular but not always reliable, especially in its translation of Paul. The New English Bible and its successor the Revised English Bible are worthy, but idiosyncratic and unreliable in places; the Jerusalem Bible and its successor the New Jerusalem Bible are sometimes brilliant but sometimes misleading. But the important thing is to get a contemporary translation and start reading it.

There are several Bible dictionaries available to help as you read: among the recent ones are the *HarperCollins Bible Dictionary* (revised edition), edited by Paul J. Achtemeier, and the *Eerdmans Dictionary of the Bible,* edited by D. N. Freedman. Two wonderful reference works which cover the massive field of the history and beliefs of the Christian church are the *Oxford Dictionary of the Christian Church* (third edition), edited by F. L. Cross and E. A. Livingstone, and the *Oxford Companion to Christian Thought,* edited by Adrian Hastings.

When it comes to the central figure of Christianity, Jesus himself, I might perhaps mention my own book *The Challenge of Jesus,* which attempts to distill the themes which I and others have worked on at a more scholarly level and to show their relevance for the task of Jesus's followers in the contemporary world.

It would be wrong, though, to give the impression that taking things further after reading this book would consist simply of reading more books. The church, for all its faults, is at its heart the community of those who are trying to follow Jesus, and in whose company those who are starting to explore these things for themselves may find help, encouragement, and wisdom. As we might say to someone starting to enjoy music: don't just listen to it, find an instrument and an orchestra and join in.